A SPECIAL PLACE

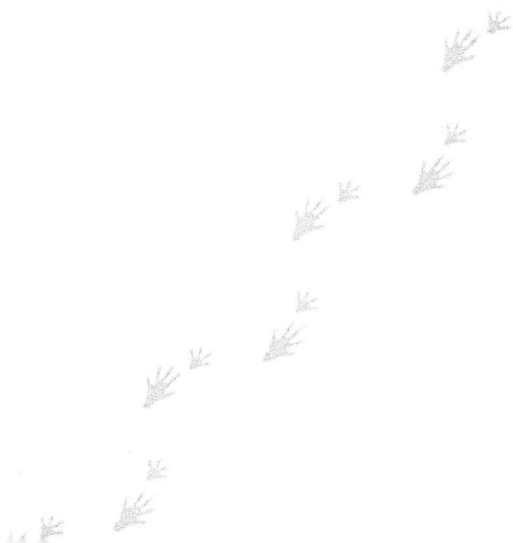

A SPECIAL PLACE

A True Account of HOA Negligence, Institutional Indifference, and Legal Failure

STEPHEN STEINER

To Rhona, Shelley, and Donna,

May life return to you the same silence, disregard,
and cruelty you so freely gave to me.

A legacy you've earned.

A proud moment indeed.

This book is not fiction.
It is not exaggerated.
It is not speculation.

Every word contained within these pages is taken directly from emails exchanged between myself, the Homeowners Association (HOA) Board Members, the property management company, the extermination companies, and the attorney I trusted to represent me.

For three years, I lived in a home that was no longer safe. A rat infestation took over the crawlspace in my condo.

Despite countless pleas for help — supported by professional inspection reports, video evidence, and health consequences — those responsible refused to act. Instead, they delayed, denied, ignored, and ultimately abandoned their duty, allowing my health, finances, and home to deteriorate.

When I hired legal counsel to protect my rights, I believed I would finally have an advocate. Instead, I encountered the same pattern of indifference and betrayal — later discovering that my attorney had a hidden prior relationship with the very law firm representing the HOA.

This book is a record of that experience.

Every email is presented exactly as it was written — unaltered, unedited, and unfiltered — to show precisely how those entrusted to protect homeowners can, through negligence and arrogance, destroy lives without ever facing accountability.

TABLE OF CONTENTS

Roof rats are aptly named for their exceptional climbing abilities, allowing them to scale walls and structures with ease. These rodents are typically dark brown or black in color and can grow to an impressive length of 12 to 18 inches, including their tails.

They are nocturnal feeders and are particularly drawn to fruit-bearing trees such as grapefruit, lemon, orange, olive, fig, and pomegranate. Beyond being a nuisance, roof rats pose a serious risk to both health and property, as they are known carriers of fleas and various diseases, and can cause significant structural damage if left unaddressed.

FOR THREE YEARS, MY HEALTH, SANITY,
AND OVERALL WELL-BEING WERE DISREGARDED
BY KEY INDIVIDUALS AND ENTITIES:

SHELLEY WESTALL
President - The Palms HOA

THE PALMS HOA BOARD OF DIRECTORS

DONNA RICKMAN
Property Manager

SEABREEZE MANAGEMENT

RHONA S. KAUFFMAN
Attorney

PREFERRED PEST CONTROL
RODENT BIRD SOLUTION
WESTERN EXTERMINATORS
NEWMAN TERMITE AND PEST CONTROL

CITY OF PALM SPRINGS

DUTIES OF THE ASSOCIATION

OPERATION AND MAINTENANCE OF COMMON AREA AND RECREATION AREA

To operate, maintain, and otherwise manage or provide for the operation,
maintenance, and management of the common area and all its facilities, improvements,
and landscaping, including any other property acquired by the Association,
in a **first-class condition** and in a good state of repair.

Source: The Palms CC&Rs

THE
BEGINNING

It all began with a single email to Donna Rickman, triggered by the sounds of a roof rat that had made its way into the crawlspace above my ceiling.

The crawlspace, which has no accessible entry from within the unit due to limited clearance—ranging from just one to two feet—is designated as a "Common Area" under the CC&Rs and is the responsibility of the HOA.

And so began a long and harrowing battle...

2022

	Mo	Tu	We	Th	Fr	Sa	Su
					1	2	3
	4	5	6	7	8	9	10
	11	12	13	14	15	16	17
	18	19	20	21	22	23	24
	25	26	27	28	29	30	31

JULY

18 DAYS UNRESOLVED

A SPECIAL PLACE

From: Stephen Steiner
To: Donna Rickman
Subject: URGENT - RODENT INVASION

JULY 14, 2022 / 9:35 PM

I am in Unit **808** and every night I hear rodents above the ceiling. Not just one but an entire community of them. They have gotten down into where my air-conditioner is located and I am afraid they will eat the wiring or cause other damage. Not to mention the rat droppings. There must be an opening on the roof for them to get in. This all started when the roof was worked on a year ago.

Is this something the HOA covers? It has become increasingly worse. I contacted the HOA back when the issue started but nothing was done.

From: Donna Rickman
To: Stephen Steiner
Subject: URGENT - RODENT INVASION

JULY 15, 2022 / 1:45 AM

I will issue a WO tomorrow morning to the pest control vendor.

From: Shonna Obeso
To: Gary Lozano
Cc: Donna Rickman
Subject: The Palms HOA Workorder - Rodents Building 800

JULY 15, 2022 / 8:39 AM

Please see attached workorder. Please advise when completed.

From: Stephen Steiner
To: Donna Rickman
Subject: URGENT - RODENT INVASION

JULY 15, 2022 / 1:25 PM

Thank you!

From: Stephen Steiner
To: Donna Rickman
Subject: Pest control and hot tub

JULY 18, 2022 / 7:49 AM

Were you able to schedule someone for my rodent problem? Let me know if you did and what time they will show up. I would like them to access the crawlspace to see if there are lots of rat droppings. I went to replace one of my ceiling bulbs and when I pulled the light fixture down a lot of droppings fell out of it.

Also, not sure if you have already been notified, the hot tub is a mess. The painters did not cover it and now there is a layer of paint floating on the top and some dead rats in it.

From: Shonna Obeso
To: Gary Lozano
Subject: The Palms HOA Workorder - Rodents Building 800

JULY 18, 2022 / 10:30 PM

Please reply to this email with updated information on this work order and when services are scheduled.

Stephen Steiner ████████████ homeowner direct phone number - please call to give information on when services are scheduled.

A SPECIAL PLACE

From: Stephen Steiner
To: Donna Rickman
Subject: Rodent Problem

Not sure what to do. The pest guy came out and checked all openings on the roof. He says it might be coming from a neighbor's unit. It is getting worse. I am up all night from the noise. It has just started again and it's only 7pm. There must be something someone can do. I will not be a happy camper if they get into my pantry or anywhere in my home.

Please contact the pest company and see if they have any ideas. I get zero sleep.

From: Donna Rickman
To: Stephen Steiner
Subject: RE: Rodent Problem

JULY 20, 2022 / 9:16 PM

I will get a follow-up report and ask what is the next step?

From: Stephen Steiner
To: Donna Rickman
Subject: Re: Rodent Problem

JULY 20, 2022 / 9:18 PM

Thanks. Ask about cleaning above the ceiling. I am sure there is an enormous amount of droppings up there and it cannot be healthy for me.

From: Donna Rickman
To: Stephen Steiner
Subject: FW: Rodent Problem

JULY 20, 2022 / 9:18 PM

Did you get the technician's name? Did he spray or lay any traps?

From: Stephen Steiner
To: Donna Rickman
Subject: Re: Rodent Problem

JULY 20, 2022 / 9:22 PM

I can get his name and don't think he did anything but check around to see if there are any openings. He did mention that if a unit is vacant for an extended amount of time the toilet water will evaporate and the rats can climb up and come out of the toilet. I know that Unit 810 (Thomas and Giuseppe) have been gone for awhile. Possibly their unit.

(See p. 76)

A SPECIAL PLACE

During the month of August, I received no updates regarding the exterminator's visit or any outlined next steps to address the ongoing rodent infestation.

The severity of the infestation continued to escalate with each passing day.

It was evident that the HOA President - Shelley Westall, Board of Directors, Donna, and Seabreeze Management showed little concern for my health or the uninhabitable conditions I was forced to endure. I have no doubt that had any of them been subjected to the same circumstances, they would have been promptly relocated to temporary housing, and the situation would have been addressed and resolved without delay.

Mo	Tu	We	Th	Fr	Sa	Su
			~~4~~	~~5~~	~~6~~	~~7~~
~~1~~	~~2~~	~~3~~	~~8~~	~~9~~	10	11
12	13	14	15	16	~~17~~	18
19	20	~~21~~	~~22~~	23	~~24~~	~~25~~
~~26~~	~~27~~	~~28~~	~~29~~	30		

SEPTEMBER

79 DAYS
UNRESOLVED

From: Stephen Steiner
  To: Donna Rickman
Subject: Rats

SEPTEMBER 7, 2022 / 1:54 AM

The rat problem is still with us. They are running all over my ceiling day and night. I still want someone to check the amount of rat droppings in the crawl space and to remove it. There must be an opening somewhere in the building.

One more thing. Can you please send out an email to all owners reminding them and their guests that the numbered parking spaces are assigned. Someone parked in my space and I had to park my car in the sun. If it is still in my space in the morning I will have it towed. Is there a tow company that The Palms uses? This could be one of the articles in the newsletter.

From: Donna Rickman
  To: Stephen Steiner
Subject: RE: Rats

SEPTEMBER 7, 2022 / 2:22 PM

What is your phone number so I can have the pest control tech contact you?

From: Stephen Steiner
  To: Donna Rickman
Subject: Re: Rats

SEPTEMBER 7, 2022 / 2:56 PM

XXXXXXXXXXXX

From: Stephen Steiner
  To: Donna Rickman
Subject: RATS

SEPTEMBER 11, 2022 / 10:08 PM

The issue is horrendous. I have video where you can hear rats running around the crawl space. It is constant all day long. Now I can see rat droppings in my light fixtures. Someone needs to come out and make a hole in the roof and gain access to the crawl space and remove all the rats and clean it up. I hear it day and night. I am scared to open my kitchen cabinets or any cabinet for fear they will jump out.

I am tired of living this way. It has gone on for so long and I guarantee living in this environment with all the rat droppings is not healthy. I also want someone to come out to check the air quality in all condos on the second floor.

Please, please, please get someone who can gain access tot he crawl space and not just walk around the building.

From: Stephen Steiner
  To: Donna Rickman
Subject: I know I am a pest

SEPTEMBER 12, 2022 / 9:53 AM

They are now in my air conditioning unit. I can hear them crawling in the tubes and one fell on the unit in my hallway. Please help.

Now I need to have the ac tubes sanitized. Please send someone out or I will find someone and have the bill sent to the HOA. I am sleeping on my couch because it is so loud with all the rats running around. I am about to go insane.

A SPECIAL PLACE

From: Donna Rickman
  To: Stephen Steiner, Giuseppe Vezzoli
Subject: PEST CONTROL

SEPTEMBER 30, 2022 / 2:11 PM

Please give me three dates and times to work with next week when you are both available
to meet the exterminator and me so I can arrange an appointment.

From: Giuseppe Vezzoli
  To: Donna Rickman, Stephen Steiner
Subject: Re: PEST CONTROL

SEPTEMBER 30, 2022 / 4:05 PM

My best date is Friday afternoon after 1:30. I can also do Saturday if that works for you.

From: Stephen Steiner
  To: Donna Rickman, Giuseppe Vezzoli
Subject: Re: PEST CONTROL

SEPTEMBER 30, 2022 / 5:18 PM

I'm open anytime.

From: Donna Rickman
  To: Stephen Steiner
  Cc: Giuseppe Vezzoli
Subject: RE: PEST CONTROL

SEPTEMBER 30, 2022 / 5:23 PM

Giuseppe mentioned he is available on Fridays after 1:30 pm. I will see if I can arrange a meeting next Friday
with the exterminator.

3 2 (See p. 76)

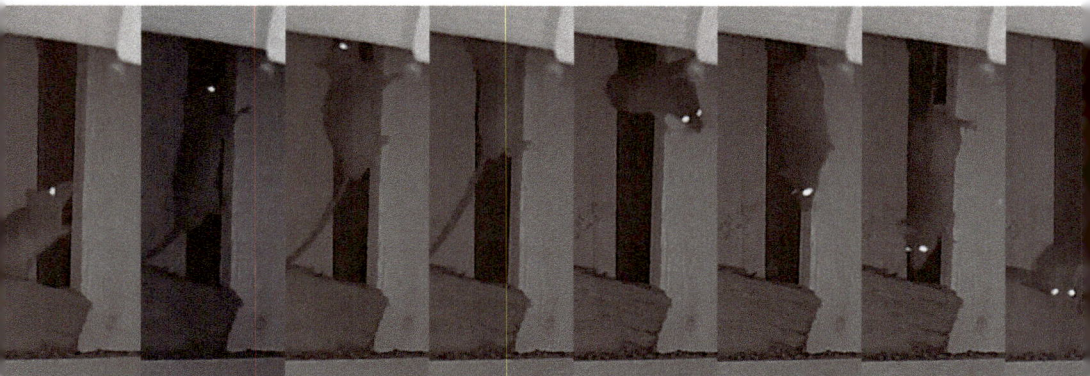

Mo	Tu	We	Th	Fr	Sa	Su
					~~X~~	~~X~~
~~X~~	~~X~~	~~X~~	~~X~~	~~X~~	~~X~~	~~X~~
10	11	12	13	14	15	16
~~17~~	~~18~~	~~19~~	~~20~~	21	~~22~~	~~23~~
~~24~~	~~25~~	~~26~~	~~27~~	~~28~~	~~29~~	~~30~~
~~31~~						

OCTOBER

110 DAYS UNRESOLVED

A SPECIAL PLACE

From: Stephen Steiner
To: Donna Rickman
Subject: Rats

OCTOBER 5, 2022 / 9:27 PM

Please have the roof opened to let out all the rats living above my ceiling. They are back and I am starting to go insane. This has to be resolved. I know you are doing your best. Living in the condo is a nightmare. The amount of poop up there must be insane. My fear is that my ceiling will have to be replaced.

From: Donna Rickman
To: Giuseppe Vezzoli
Subject: PEST CONTROL APPOINTMENT

OCTOBER 6, 2022 / 1:50 PM

The pest control appointment is arranged for tomorrow, Friday, at 3:00 pm. Please confirm.

From: Stephen Steiner
To: Donna Rickman
Cc: Giuseppe Vezzoli
Subject: Re: PEST CONTROL APPOINTMENT

OCTOBER 6, 2022 / 1:58 PM

I confirm.

From: Donna Rickman
To: Stephen Steiner
Cc: Giuseppe Vezzoli
Subject: Re: PEST CONTROL APPOINTMENT

OCTOBER 6, 2022 / 1:59 PM

Thank you, Stephen!

From: Stephen Steiner
To: Donna Rickman
Cc: Giuseppe Vezzoli
Subject: Re: PEST CONTROL APPOINTMENT

OCTOBER 6, 2022 / 2:03 PM

You are welcome and thank you for arranging it. I am attaching a photo of the pine tree that either needs to be trimmed back or removed.

From: Giuseppe Vezzoli
To: Donna Rickman
Cc: Stephen Steiner
Subject: Re: PEST CONTROL APPOINTMENT

OCTOBER 6, 2022 / 2:10 PM

I will be there.

From: Donna Rickman
To: Giuseppe Vezzoli
Cc: Stephen Steiner
Subject: Re: PEST CONTROL APPOINTMENT

OCTOBER 6, 2022 / 2:23 PM

Great, see you then.

EASY
ROOF ACCESS
FOR RATS

A SPECIAL PLACE

From: Donna Rickman
To: Stephen Steiner
Subject: Rats

OCTOBER 7, 2022 / 2:51 PM

Running a little later.

From: Stephen Steiner
To: Donna Rickman
Subject: Re: Rats

OCTOBER 7, 2022 / 2:56 PM

No problem, see you when you get here.

From: Donna Rickman
To: Stephen Steiner
Subject: Rats

OCTOBER 7, 2022 / 2:57 PM

I will be there about 3:20.

From: Donna Rickman
To: Stephen Steiner
Subject: Fwd: Rats

OCTOBER 7, 2022 / 3:26 PM

What's your unit number?

From: Stephen Steiner
To: Donna Rickman
Subject: Exterminator

OCTOBER 13, 2022 / 8:38 PM

It was a pleasure meeting you in person. Just checking to see when the exterminator will be coming to open up the ceiling. I am also attaching a PDF of what is currently in the crawlspace.

Donna met with Giuseppe and me inside my condo to discuss the installation of a crawlspace access panel. We walked through each room to determine the best possible location. She was very complimentary on my decor and noted how exceptionally clean the condo was.

I told her many times I did not want the access panel installed inside my home and requested it be placed on the roof instead. This would have eliminated the need for exterminators to repeatedly enter my living space. She refused, claiming it would void the roof warranty. I urged her to contact the roofing company, as the roof had been replaced just a year prior and was likely the source of the infestation.

During the walk through, I mentioned that I planned to create a small hole in the ceiling and install a webcam to document the extent of the rat activity in the crawlspace. Donna quickly informed me that the crawlspace was HOA property and that any such action was strictly prohibited. She reminded me several times that I was not to access the crawlspace.

LAUNDRY & HALLWAY CEILING LIGHTS

(See p. 76)

Interior ceiling light fixtures include two located in the hallway and one in the laundry. All three fixtures are in close proximity to one another and covered in rodent feces. The fixture in the laundry area is positioned directly above the dryer, where the rodents had constructed a substantial nest. All three were shown to Donna and the extermination company during their visit.

CDC Centers for Disease Control and Prevention

HEALTH THREATS FROM RODENT INFESTATION

Rat infestations and human contact with rats can cause health problems, problems with contamination, and damage to property.

The United States Centers for Disease Control and Prevention lists several diseases that can be caused by rats:

HANTAVIRUS PULMONARY SYNDROME (HPS):
An often deadly disease transmitted by rodents through urine, feces, or saliva. Humans can contract the disease when they breathe in dried, aerosolized secretions. Although a rare disease, the severity of the infection underscores reason for concern. Rodent control in and around the home is the best method of prevention.

SEOUL VIRUS AND HANTAVIRUS FEVER WITH RENAL SYNDROME (HFRS):
The natural hosts of Seoul virus are the Norway rat (Rattus norvegicus) and the black or "roof" rat (Rattus rattus), very common rats in Louisiana; however, Seoul virus occurs worldwide. Rats do not get sick with this virus, but, when infected, they shed the virus their entire lives. Most people infected with Seoul virus either do not get sick at all, or exhibit mild flu-like symptoms. A small minority of cases will develop the most severe form of the disease, referred to as HFRS. HFRS affects the kidneys and can cause hemorrhagic fever. Approximately 1% to 2% of people who develop HFRS will die. Seoul virus is transmitted in much the same way as other Hantaviruses, primarily through exposure to rodent urine, feces or nesting materials that are stirred up, often while cleaning. Rodent control and prevention of exposure to dangerous materials are the best means of prevention.

MURINE TYPHUS:
This disease occurs worldwide, but is rather rare in the Americas, and is transmitted to humans by rat fleas. The disease is more common in the summer months, but in warmer climates, can occur throughout the year. Rat-infested buildings and homes, especially in port or riverine environments, are often havens for rats harboring infected fleas. The etiologic agents are Streptobacillus moniliformis and Spirillum minus.

RAT-BITE FEVER:
This is a systemic bacterial illness that can be transmitted from rats to humans through a bite, a scratch, or through the ingestion of food and water contaminated with rat feces. Approximately one out of every ten persons who contracts the disease will die.

SALMONELLA ENTERICA SEROVAR TYPHIMURIUM:
This bacterium does not normally cause serious illness in humans, although an infection can be characterized by diarrhea, abdominal cramps, vomiting and nausea. However in the elderly, the very young or in people with reduced immunity, Salmonella infections can be fatal.

LEPTOSPIROSIS:
Caused by Leptospira bacteria. Infection with this organism can result in a range of symptoms, from no illness at all to mild symptoms (headache, fever, abdominal pain, diarrhea, rash) to severe disease resulting in kidney damage, meningitis, liver failure, and respiratory distress. These infections are sometimes fatal.

EOSINOPHILIC MENINGITIS:
Sometimes results from infection of the brain with stages of the rat lungworm, Angiostrongylus cantonensis. Some infected people don't have any symptoms -- or have only mild symptoms that don't last very long. Sometimes the infection causes eosinophilic meningitis. The symptoms can include headache, stiff neck, tingling or painful feelings in the skin, low-grade fever, nausea, and vomiting. Symptoms can last from several weeks to months.

Rats can produce up to 12 to 16 milliliters (more than 2 teaspoons – more than 1 tablespoon) of urine and 50 fecal droppings in a 24-hour period. Contamination of stored foods with rodent feces and urine may transmit disease to both humans and pets. These contaminated foods may carry diseases such as cryptosporidiosis, toxoplasmosis, leptospirosis, salmonellosis, and listeriosis. In addition to causing disease, contamination from rat urine and droppings increases spoilage and renders foods inedible.

Rats have also been implicated in the transmission of several other helminths (worms) and bacterial, rickettsial, protozoal, and viral infections in other parts of the world. Rat lice, mites, and fleas can also infest other animals and, occasionally, people.

Rats can also cause considerable damage to property and buildings. An example of this is the gnawing of electrical cables.

A SPECIAL PLACE

This health advisory document outlines the severe health hazards associated with prolonged rodent infestations—particularly the toxic consequences of exposure to rat feces and urine in a sealed environment like my crawlspace. According to the CDC, a single rat can produce over 50 fecal droppings and more than a tablespoon of urine per day, all capable of transmitting serious and potentially fatal diseases, including Hantavirus, Leptospirosis, Salmonella, Rat-Bite Fever, and eosinophilic meningitis. By the time I submitted this document, over four months had passed with no meaningful intervention. The infestation had worsened significantly, and yet, despite this clear and medically recognized danger, no one—Shelley Westall, the HOA Board of Directors, Donna Rickman, or Seabreeze Management—took action to relocate me or address the crisis with any urgency.

What was most devastating was not just the toxic environment I was forced to endure, but the complete and deliberate indifference shown by every party responsible. I was paying $460 per month in HOA dues, which explicitly includes maintenance of common areas and reasonable action in the event of a health hazard. Every exterminator who entered my home warned of the dangers, and still, I was left to live in conditions that no human being should ever be subjected to. The proper legal and ethical response would have been immediate relocation and full remediation. Instead, I was abandoned.

The psychological toll was immense and ongoing. I suffered repeated outbreaks of shingles due to stress, insomnia, anxiety, and ultimately developed Bell's palsy. I was living in constant fear—surrounded by the stench of decay, the scratching of rodents above my head, and the knowledge that those in charge simply didn't care. Their refusal to act wasn't just negligent—it was inhumane. I trusted that my rights would be upheld, that someone would intervene. Instead, my trust was weaponized against me.

Their behavior was calculated, cruel, and entirely self-serving—motivated not by duty or decency, but by a desire to avoid the cost of repairs. They treated my suffering as an inconvenience and allowed my health to collapse in pursuit of financial self-preservation. If this had happened to one of them or their loved ones, the response would have been immediate and aggressive. But in my case, they chose silence, delay, and willful inaction.

My greatest mistake was believing they would do the right thing. What they did instead was a betrayal of both legal obligation and basic human compassion.

From: Donna Rickman
To: Stephen Steiner
Cc: Giuseppe Vezzoli
Subject: RE: Exterminator

OCTOBER 14, 2022 / 10:55 AM

I am coordinating the estimate for the 2'x 2' cut and service door with the handyman. According to the responsibility matrix, the cut and service door is the homeowner responsibility. However, the HOA will pay for the inspection and traps.

I should have the estimate to you late today. I am shooting for Monday to have the cut and service door installed if you and Dr. Vezzoli agree to the estimate. Then next Tuesday, the traps set. Please let me know your thoughts.

From: Stephen Steiner
To: Donna Rickman
Cc: Giuseppe Vezzoli
Subject: Re: Exterminator

OCTOBER 14, 2022 / 12:51 PM

This is why I wanted the opening to be on the roof. I did not want the responsibility to pay for any of this since the rats were coming in from the roof. With my luck, I will end up having to pay for everything which I refuse to do. I will wait for the estimate before I make a decision.

From: Donna Rickman
To: Stephen Steiner, Giuseppe Vezzoli
Subject: FW: 2'x2' access panels

OCTOBER 14, 2022 / 1:48 PM

Hi Stephen and Giuseppe, please see the estimate below from Cory. For a cut and service door that will be permanent, this is a very reasonable cost.

Please let me know what you think.

A SPECIAL PLACE

From: Corey Mckeown
To: Donna Rickman
Subject: FW: 2'x2' access panels

OCTOBER 14, 2022 / 11:25 AM

The cost per access hole would be approximately $250 each. Being that this estimate is being done site unseen, the price is subject to change.

The holes could be cut upon acceptance of the estimate. And the actual access panels would be ordered immediately thereafter. And you take approximately 3 to 5 business days to arrive.

We also request a 50% down payment to begin the work. This is to help cover the material costs. And we would also require an agreement of payment in full at the time of job completion.

From: Stephen Steiner
To: Donna Rickman
Cc: Giuseppe Vezzoli
Subject: Re: 2'x 2' access panels

OCTOBER 14, 2022 / 2:46 PM

Giuseppe, I will let them put the traps on your side. I don't think I can take another week of smelling rats decomposing. I have been suffering with this situation for so long that I think that smell will throw me off the edge I am already starting to fall over.

From: Stephen Steiner
To: Donna Rickman
Cc: Giuseppe Vezzoli
Subject: Re: 2'x2' access panels

OCTOBER 14, 2022 / 8:43 PM

What was the reason for not going through the roof? I do not want to pay for any of this because it came from outside and not from inside the units. This was also just an estimate. I guarantee it will cost more. I am already paying $430 a month for HOA dues. It is a cost that the homeowner should not be required to pay. Please notify the Board and send them the attachment of what we all have been exposed to. This will convince them to have the roof opened.

From: Donna Rickman
To: Stephen Steiner
Cc: Giuseppe Vezzoli
Subject: Re: 2'x2' access panels

OCTOBER 14, 2022 / 8:50 PM

I will get an estimate from the roof vendor so we will have a comparison of the estimates. In the meantime, I will forward your concerns and get an answer on how the board would like to proceed.

From: Stephen Steiner
To: Donna Rickman
Cc: Giuseppe Vezzoli
Subject: Re: 2'x2' access panels

OCTOBER 14, 2022 / 9:16 PM

Thanks, Donna. I have also noticed what appears to be moisture on all my walls and my carpeting throughout the unit is all warping. I hope the rats did not make holes in the pipes and it is leaking slowly under my carpeting.

The padding I had installed under the carpeting has a plastic layer on top so that if something is spilled it will not penetrate the foam padding. I think that all the moisture is coming up where it meets the walls and is able to evaporate.

People have noticed that it seems mushy and has a moldy smell. It was not this way 7 months ago. I had to go through the unit and wipe all marks of water running down the wall near the baseboards.

Is it possible for someone to contact the owner downstairs and find out if they are having any issues in their unit?

The rats have destroyed my home, and I am pretty sure it is unsafe to live in.

Have a great weekend and sorry for all my ranting. I think the Hantavirus is slowly driving me insane.

A SPECIAL PLACE

From: Donna Rickman
To: Stephen Steiner
Cc: Giuseppe Vezzoli
Subject: RE: Exterminator

I just talked with Corey and the service door has to be ordered, but he said the approximate cost will be around $250.00, which includes the door. I will send you the formal estimate later today. Let's discuss then.

This situation was both infuriating and deeply troubling. On one hand, Donna had explicitly instructed me not to create any openings in the ceiling, stating that it was HOA property and therefore outside my authority to modify. Yet, despite that clear position, I was later informed that I would be financially responsible for installing an access panel in that same HOA-controlled property. This blatant contradiction reflects not only a complete lack of consistency and oversight, but a pattern of incompetence and mismanagement that placed both my property and health at continued risk.

From: Giuseppe Vezzoli
To: Stephen Steiner
Cc: Donna Rickman
Subject: Re: 2'x2' access panels

I just read your emails. As Steve said I would like to send all this info to the board. Although we are responsible for the ceiling, we are not responsible for the incompetence of the pest control company if they can't figure where and how the rats get into the building. The incompetence of someone else that is causing damage to our units and health shouldn't come to our expenses.

From: Stephen Steiner
To: Donna Rickman
Cc: Giuseppe Vezzoli
Subject: URGENT!!! ANOTHER MAJOR ISSUE!!

Big problem. I noticed that over the year water stains have appeared on the walls. I began wiping them down and realized the rats must have made a hole in a pipe and the water is flowing down and being absorbed into the padding of my carpet. That is why my carpet has become loose and appears as though it is wet. My unit has become very humid and smells rancid. Every week that goes buy it gets worse.

This situation raised serious health and legal concerns, as my entire condo began showing prominent yellow staining on the interior walls. Given the prolonged negligence by Shelley Westali, Donna Rickman, Seabreeze Management, and the HOA Board of Directors, and the persistent, overwhelming odor throughout the unit, I had legitimate reason to believe that the stains were the result of prolonged exposure to rodent feces and urine—specifically, airborne particulates originating from saturated insulation in the HOA-owned crawlspace.

It is critical to note that the area infested was not part of my individual unit, but rather common area property under the legal responsibility of the HOA. Their failure to remediate the infestation allowed toxins to permeate my living space, creating conditions that were both unsafe and inhumane.

Several years prior, a similar issue arose when the homeowner below me alleged a leak was coming from my unit. I acted responsibly and hired a licensed plumber to investigate. His assessment conclusively determined that the leak originated from the unit below—not mine. Despite my attempts to communicate these findings, the downstairs neighbor continued to blame me until the plumber's inspection of their unit confirmed the true source.

In the current situation, I again sought a professional opinion. The plumber evaluated the staining and dampness and noted that while Palm Springs' rising humidity—exacerbated by over development and changes in climate—may contribute to condensation, the pattern, color, and location of the yellow staining were more consistent with the breakdown of biological waste, specifically rodent urine and feces. This was further supported by the thermal imaging I provided to the HOA, which clearly showed areas of contamination directly above the stained walls.

From: Donna Rickman
To: Stephen Steiner, Giuseppe Vezzoli
Subject: Re: URGENT!!! ANOTHER MAJOR ISSUE!!

Trying to arrange a plumber to come over in the morning. I will contact the units below you tomorrow morning if I have their contact information. Always leave your unit number in case I'm not by my computer. I'm schedule to be on-site for a landscape walk at 8:00 am. If the HOA pays for the cut and service door, will you allow the cut from the inside of your unit?

A SPECIAL PLACE

From: Stephen Steiner
  To: Donna Rickman
  Cc: Giuseppe Vezzoli
Subject: Handyman

OCTOBER 19, 2022 / 10:58 AM

Handyman did not show up yesterday. Will he be coming today?

From: Donna Rickman
  To: Stephen Steiner
  Cc: Giuseppe Vezzoli
Subject: RE: Handyman

OCTOBER 19, 2022 / 11:12 AM

The plumber showed up yesterday. I am still waiting for board approval.

From: Donna Rickman
  To: Stephen Steiner, Giuseppe Vezzoli
Subject: FW: Handyman

OCTOBER 23, 2022 / 11:38 AM

Good morning, Stephen, and Giuseppe:

Yesterday, I was directed by the Board to obtain a second opinion. Therefore, I would like to schedule an appointment this week with another pest control provider.

Stephen, when are you available this week?

Giuseppe, do you mind if Stephen lets the pest control into your unit?

After the second opinion, we will be able to move forward. Thank you for your patience.

From: Giuseppe Vezzoli
  To: Donna Rickman, Stephen Steiner
Subject: Re: Handyman

OCTOBER 23, 2022 / 11:50 AM

Stephen has the key and he can come into my condo when the other pest control person decides to come. Thank you Donna.

From: Stephen Steiner
  To: Donna Rickman
  Cc: Giuseppe Vezzoli
Subject: Re: Handyman

OCTOBER 23, 2022 / 7:28 PM

Second opinion to drag this out even longer?

Do they realize I have been living with rats for the past year and a half. Even you have seen the droppings in my light fixtures. I wish I could dump all the rat feces and urine into their homes and tell them they need a second opinion.

The rats are still here and I hear them every night. I am going nuts just sitting and waiting for something to be done. It is though nobody cares that I am living with this situation. Week after week goes by and nothing gets done. I just want this to be over so I can move on.

Please schedule another pest control provider as soon as you can so I can wait another couple weeks for a decision to be made and delay the process even more.

	Mo	Tu	We	Th	Fr	Sa	Su
	X	X	X	X	X	X
X	X	X	10	11	12	13
14	15	16	17	18	19	20
X	X	X	24	X	X	X
X	X	X				

NOVEMBER

140 DAYS
UNRESOLVED

A SPECIAL PLACE

From: Stephen Steiner
To: Donna Rickman
Subject: Exterminator

NOVEMBER 8, 2022 / 6:23 PM

I heard the quote was approved. When are they scheduled to make the opening?

I would like it done as soon as possible as well as the cleanup. I would like to get my property ready to sell as soon as possible.

From: Donna Rickman
To: Stephen Steiner
Subject: Re: Exterminator

NOVEMBER 8, 2022 / 6:24 PM

Just waiting for the access doors to be delivered.

From: Donna Rickman
To: Stephen Steiner
Cc: Giuseppe Vezzoli
Subject: FW: Exterminator

NOVEMBER 14, 2022 / 11:11 AM

Are you available today between 10:30 and 11:00 for the access door installation? If not, please let me know when you are available.

(See p. 76) (See p. 76)

Two handymen and an exterminator arrived at my condo to install the crawlspace access panel.

However, rather than providing a proper access door, Donna delivered a heavy metal breaker panel—an item clearly not designed or suitable for ceiling installation. It became apparent that no legitimate attempt had been made to acquire the correct access panel. Given that a standard access panel could have been easily and inexpensively obtained from a Home Depot located less than ten minutes from the property, it is reasonable to conclude that no such order was ever placed.

The substitution of a breaker panel—an item with an entirely different function—reflects either gross incompetence or intentional obstruction. Any reasonable person would understand that a breaker panel is wholly incompatible with the intended purpose. This decision cannot be seen as a mere oversight. Rather, when viewed in context with the broader pattern of conduct, it suggests a deliberate effort to delay resolution and exacerbate my hardship. Taken together with prior actions, it is reasonable to infer that both Shelley and Donna acted in bad faith and may have taken some measure of satisfaction in obstructing the process and prolonging my suffering.

We continued to evaluate possible locations for the access point, and I recommended the laundry closet ceiling above the washer and dryer. It was the most logical option, as the rats had built a nest around the warm exhaust pipe during the winter months. Despite my input, the decision was made to proceed with the installation in the primary bedroom closet ceiling. Once the opening was made, it quickly became apparent that access was blocked by pipes and electrical wiring.

Uncertain how to proceed, the workers contacted Donna. I reiterated my suggestion to use the laundry area, but she instructed them to seal the hole and revisit the project at a later date. The patchwork was done hastily and never properly completed. Before it was sealed, I used my cellphone to document the condition of the crawlspace on video.

Furthermore, the 14-day delay in approving the access panel installation was entirely unjustified. The matter could have been resolved with a single phone call to Shelley Westall. Both Shelley and Donna willfully and unnecessarily prolonged the process, reflecting a complete disregard for proper planning and a lack of respect for my property, which my partner and I had recently invested significant time and resources to remodel. The extensive presence of rat feces should have immediately raised serious concerns regarding not only my individual unit, but the health and safety of all residents within the 800 building. Despite being directly informed by exterminators that the unit was toxic, both Shelley and Donna continued to demonstrate willful indifference and negligence in addressing the severity of the infestation.

A SPECIAL PLACE

From: Giuseppe Vezzoli
  To: Donna Rickman
  Cc: Stephen Steiner
Subject: Rat Issues

NOVEMBER 16, 2022 / 1:07 AM

Good morning Donna,

I assume you saw the video of Stephen's attic conditions, if you haven't seen it, the video is attached to this email with the video of the noise above my kitchen as well. Most likely my unit is in the same condition with rat droppings and urine just above our heads. Not only, it's gross and disgusting, but as you are well aware it is very UNHEALTHY. Clearly the exterminator we have is incompetent. There are different possibilities to take care of rats, if he is unable to do it we have to hire someone else IMMEDIATELY, not next year after the board meeting. This should be a PRIORITY, I repeat this is a HEALTHY ISSUE, rat urine impregnating the ceiling is unhealthy. Lights and painting can wait. As you know when rats find a way in, they can reproduce and make lovely homes, something we should avoid.

Steve and I have been VERY patients with our "friends" above our heads and the board members. However, apparently the board and the HOA doesn't care that much. I urge you to forward this email and the videos to the board members (I know some of these people don't live here and perhaps don't care, WE DO!!!). Perhaps we can move into their condo when this is being taken care of? What do you think?

I guess if no one will proceed to take care of this issue we will proceed with more competent contractors, control-rodent people and attic cleaning companies. We will be pleased then to send our bills to the HOA.

From: Donna Rickman
  To: Giuseppe Vezzoli
  Cc: Stephen Steiner
Subject: Re: rat issues

NOVEMBER 16, 2022 / 1:20 AM

Everything is approved. The problem yesterday was finding a place in the ceiling without air ducts and pipes. Jordan is meeting with handyman at 11:30 am tomorrow.

From: Stephen Steiner
  To: Donna Rickman
  Cc: Giuseppe Vezzoli
Subject: More rats

NOVEMBER 16, 2022 / 12:28 AM

New family of rats moved in. They are extremely loud and running around the entire ceiling. I have attached a video.

From: Donna Rickman
  To: Stephen Steiner
  Cc: Giuseppe Vezzoli, Shonna Obeso
Subject: RATS IN THE CEILINGS

NOVEMBER 16, 2022 / 7:23 PM

Today, myself and Jordan from Preferred Pest Control met to install the access door in your primary bedroom so Jordan could set the rat traps. I also brought over a worker from Vantage Construction to install the access door so that the rat traps could be placed in the ceiling. After the worker reviewed the cut that was made and temporarily closed on Monday, 11/14/2022, he said the door needed a frame to secure the door on the ceiling. I offered to go to Home Depot to buy a 2 X 4 so he could install the access door today. However, you stated that you were overwhelmed and didn't like the access door location in your closet.

You also stated that you will install an access door that is plastic in a location somewhere in your bedroom, preferably the wall above the entry door into the bedroom or just to the right of the door. Jordan from Preferred Pest Control said that the location would work if the cut was not obstructed by air ducts or pipes. You also stated that you will install the door by this Friday, 11/18,2022. It is understood that this door is temporary, and the wall will be returned to its original state after the rat problem has been resolved.

Stephen if you change your mind, please let me know and I will schedule someone again to install the access door.

As can be seen in the correspondence, the tone of Donna Rickman's emails shifted markedly, likely in response to internal reprimands for her gross mishandling of this matter. Shelley Westall,, who was directly involved alongside Ms. Rickman, demonstrated a similar failure in judgment and competence. Ms. Westall's complete detachment—residing neither in the complex nor even in the same state—left her entirely unaware of the severity and escalating nature of the rodent infestation.

Despite my repeated and well-documented efforts to convey the seriousness of the situation, the HOA Board, Seabreeze Management, and their representatives consistently downplayed the problem, treating it as an isolated incident rather than the systemic infestation it was. My concerns were repeatedly dismissed, and no meaningful action was taken. Had Seabreeze Management, Ms. Rickman, or Ms. Westall exercised even minimal due diligence—such as engaging the roofing company or placing proper rooftop traps—the extensive damages and prolonged health risks could have been avoided.

From: Donna Rickman
To: Stephen Steiner
Cc: Giuseppe Vezzoli
Subject: FW: RATS IN THE CEILINGS

NOVEMBER 17, 2022 / 7:48 PM

Please confirm that you are taking responsibility to install the access door at a location of your choice and that you declined the help from the HOA. Of course, the HOA will still provide the rat abatement services.

This email was both contradictory and nonsensical. According to the CC&Rs, as well as prior statements from Donna and the HOA, I was expressly prohibited from accessing or modifying HOA property. Yet, in this instance, Donna suddenly expressed no objection to me installing an access panel myself. This reversal of position highlights the inconsistency and lack of coherent decision-making throughout the process.

Moreover, I had repeatedly advised that the access panel should be installed on the roof—an approach that would have directly addressed the rodent entry point. The refusal to follow that recommendation, coupled with shifting instructions, suggests yet another intentional delay. The continued mismanagement and lack of accountability were not only frustrating but deeply concerning.

From: Stephen Steiner
To: Donna Rickman
Cc: Giuseppe Vezzoli, Shonna Obeso
Subject: Re: RATS IN THE CEILINGS

NOVEMBER 18, 2022 / 4:11 AM

I am confused by your email. It is written as though I am the one delaying this process.

On 11/14/2022 the handyman arrived at 10am and did not complete the project till 4:30pm.

The original hole that was made for installing the trap door was not planned well. No one took time to research what was above the drywall. Corey, the handyman, was told to make a hole in the primary bedroom closet because the exterminator suggested this location. If the exterminator had used an infrared gun similar to the one the plumber used to check for water leaks due to the condensation on all my interior walls. It would have shown the pipe directly above the drywall. Because a better location for the hole was needed, the handyman and I contacted you and sent pictures with a markup of the new location for approval. Since a decision could not be made until Jordan approved of the new location, the project was canceled and the hole was patched.

The trap doors that were ordered are not suited for this project. They are used for electrical boxes on a vertical wall. The doors are heavy and need to be attached to a wooden frame. With the correct trap door and location this would have been a one hour project instead of a six hour project. My entire day was wasted not to mention the handyman's. The only positive is the video footage of the rat droppings on the ceiling.

On 11/16/2022 at 12pm Jordan, his boss and you arrived at my condo to find a new place to install the trap door. After discussing with Jordan, a decision was made to reopen the previous hole, add a wooden frame, and attach the trap door. A worker from Vantage Construction was brought over to install the door. He was given quick instructions of what needed to be done. After you left the room I asked if he understood the task. He did not understand the previous hole needed to be reopened and a frame built to support the trap door. He was going to screw the door directly to the drywall with no opening. That is why I volunteered to do the installation. Not because I wanted to do it but because it seems that no one really cares. Everything is done on a whim with people who are not experienced.

A SPECIAL PLACE

I have been suffering through this ordeal since the first email I sent to you on July 14, 2022 at 9:35pm.

> Hi Donna,
>
> I am in Unit 808 and every night I hear rodents above the ceiling. Not just one but an entire community of them. They have gotten down into where my air-conditioner is located and I am afraid they will eat the wiring or cause other damage. Not to mention the rat droppings. There must be an opening on the roof for them to get in. This all started when the roof was worked on a year ago. Is this something the HOA covers? It has become increasingly worse. I contacted the HOA back when the issue started but nothing was done.
>
> Please let me know as soon as possible. I want to avoid any expensive repairs.

It has been over 5 months dealing with the rodent invasion. I am at a loss conveying the amount of stress, disgust, sleepless nights, and health hazard this has caused. Inhaling all the particles from the urine and droppings more than likely has affected my health and those in the 800 building. I get very little sleep and if I do it is on the couch with all the lights on. Opening any closet or cabinet causes me an immense amount of anxiety. These are not small rats or just one rat. There are many and they are large and create an enormous amount of noise. This should have been taken care of the day after my email and continued until resolved. I have emailed numerous times in July, August, September, October, and November and the problem still continues. Jordan has sealed all holes, the other exterminator has checked, and the plumber has checked. Everything is sealed but the rats are still entering. The pine tree hanging over the roof is possibly another way for them to get access to the roof.

Overwhelmed is an understatement. I am mentally destroyed. I am in constant fear the rats will find a way in. They can chew on electrical wires or pipes and cause an extraordinary amount of damage. My home is no longer a home. It is a place that I feel disgusted and uncomfortable living in. I do not want my unit to become "Trap Central". I am not happy that this has been dropped mostly on my shoulders. I have been patient and flexible for many months and nothing has been accomplished.

A trap door for each unit should be installed on the roof. It would allow access at anytime without inconveniencing the owner. When I mentioned this you, stated that it would void the warranty. So that makes the roof more important than the well-being of the homeowners? I guarantee the roofing company would have a solution to work around this. As for the clean up, I do not want a crew of people dragging their equipment and chemicals throughout my home. It should all be done from the roof.

I have decided I do not want any trap door installed. This is an 800 building issue the HOA needs to resolve. Unless the entry point is located and sealed this will continue. I do not have the stomach to listen to an animal suffer (even rats), not to mention the stench from a decomposing rodent.

You will have to find another way or another unit. If they are in my crawl space they are in everyones crawl space.

Due to the manner in which Donna composed her final email—written in a style noticeably different from her previous correspondence, leading me to strongly suspect that Shelley was involved in drafting or influencing its content—I made a deliberate effort to document my subsequent emails thoroughly, including specific names, dates, times, and actions.

From: Donna Rickman
To: Stephen Steiner
Subject: FW: RATS IN THE CEILINGS

NOVEMBER 28, 2022 / 5:51 PM

The Board, this morning, past a comprehensive plan for eradicating the rats. Please see attached plan that was approve by the Board of Directors this morning. After you read the plan, please let me know if we can have your permission to place a trap door as indicated in the proposal. The company has their own in-house people install the doors. The doors would be temporary and after the rates are eradicated, the area would be restored to its original condition. I can have the point person for the project contact you if you have any questions. I believe we can have someone scheduled for this Thursday if you are available.

Also, the Board rejects going through the roof as a solution because of warranty issues, possible water leaks and expense.

Western Exterminator Company
A Rentokil Steritech Company
Your Local Pest Control Experts

Proposal for Service: Rodent Prevention and Control

The Palms HOA
3155 Ramon Road Building 800
Palm Springs, CA 9226

Prepared by: Shane Norwood

Overview

This presentation will provide you with our proposal to proactively protect your facility from rodent activity and eliminate the current rodent infestation at building 800. The recommended options include rodent exclusion, to provide an intensive rodent trapping program, and the addition of exterior rodent bait stations. This proposal is outlined and illustrated in this presentation.

Should you have any questions please contact me at:

Shane Norwood
(714) 262-1876
Shane.Norwood@west-ext.com

Three Reasons To Take Action:

#1 – Human Health

RODENT-BORNE DISEASES

TYPES OF DISEASES
- SALMONELLOSIS
- LEPTOSPIROSIS
- PLAGUE
- WEIL'S DISEASE
- RAT BITE FEVER
- HANATAVIRUS

SIGNS OF INFECTION

| CHEST PAINS | NAUSEA OR VOMITING | FEVER | CHILLS | RASH |

Three Reasons To Take Action:

#2 – Safety and structure

Rodents often chew through wires, drywall, hard plastic, and rubber to file down their teeth.

Roof Rats

Roof rats are common in the area and are prone to infest any structure that is left open for them. These rats can fit into any size opening the size of a quarter or larger, it is important to have your structure fully rodent excluded in order to assure full rodent eradication. Once inside the structure it is within the rodents nature to live up high like the attic or roof void areas, this is why we need access to these areas in order to provide the proper rodent trapping measures. Once inside female rodents can have 3-6 litters of 6-8 pups within a years time span.

We Conducted a Detailed Rodent Inspection and Found Activity in the Following Areas

Unit 808 is hearing rodent activity within the ceiling void area and fresh roof rat droppings can be found within the interior Air Conditioning closet.

A SPECIAL PLACE

We Conducted a Detailed Rodent Inspection and Found Activity in the Following Areas

Within unit 810 fresh rodent droppings and urine can be found within the cabinet above the stove and under the kitchen sink.

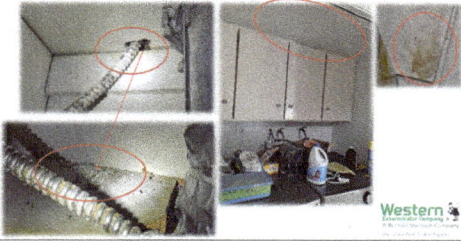

In order to solve the problem we will need to perform some rodent exclusion

This light fixture outside of unit 810, electrical outlet outside of unit 807, and the opening within the back electrical closet behind unit 805 are in need of rodent exclusion in order to assure full rodent eradication.

In order to solve the problem we will need to perform some rodent exclusion

There is an opening within this electrical room that is in need of rodent exclusion in order to assure full rodent eradication.

We Recommend To fully Rodent Exclude All Openings Found Around The Building

We will be using special Rodent Excluder material

We recommend to set up a 3 week intensive rodent trapping program

Set Up Trapping Program

We recommend setting up traps inside the affected areas 12 units and ceiling to capture any rodents which access/currently inhabit the areas. These traps will be checked weekly (3 times per week for 3 weeks) until we capture all rodents inside. The exclusion work will prevent new issues after this.

Access Points For Trapping

We recommend for us to provide an access point in the ceiling of the laundry room for the 6 units that are effected.

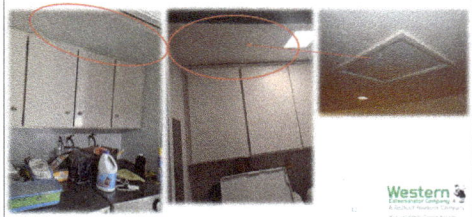

We Recommend the Installation of 8 Exterior Rodent Bait Stations

Bait Stations are a good first line of defense, as the rodents travel the edge of the wall they will enter into one of our bait stations where the rodent will find and eat poison before attempting to enter your facility.

Investment Details

Services	Price
To provide rodent exclusion using our rodent excluder line of products for the following locations, 2 stucco openings, light fixture opening, and 2 separate back electrical closet openings.	$265
To provide a 3 week intensive rodent trapping program to consist of setting up rodent traps within the ceiling void areas of 12 units and to provide check backs 3 times a week for a period of 3 weeks. If need be we will continue to trap until all rodents are trapped within the building at no additional charge.	$1,193
To provide a ceiling void access point in the laundry room of 6 units.	$2,160
To provide the installation of 8 exterior rodent bait stations.	$152
Total Cost of Services:	**$3,770**

A SPECIAL PLACE

A PowerPoint presentation was prepared by Western Exterminator Company and presented to the Board of Directors during an HOA meeting. It served no legitimate purpose and accomplished nothing, other than confirming the serious health risks associated with living amidst the infestation. It was clearly intended to create further delays and add to my frustration.

As documented in slide three, there were numerous reasons requiring immediate action. I was deeply concerned, as nearly five months had passed without any meaningful remediation. My condominium was filled with a persistent, foul odor, and rats had already fallen onto the air conditioning unit located in the hallway closet. The exterminators had identified a large opening on the roof, yet failed to seal it — raising serious concerns that they may have been instructed or encouraged not to do so. To this day, I have no certainty that any of the openings were ever properly sealed.

Donna's reasoning for not addressing the issue through the roof was completely unfounded. Placing traps on the roof would have been the most effective approach, as it would have identified the entry point and discouraged the rodents from entering the crawlspace. Instead, placing food and traps directly inside the crawlspace only served to attract more rodents into the unit, further exacerbating the problem.

From: Giuseppe Vezzoli
    To: Donna Rickman
    Bcc: Stephen Steiner
Subject: Re: Board approved Rat Exclusion Plan

NOVEMBER 28, 2022 / 11:34 PM

I hope you had a lovely Thanksgiving as well.

Unfortunately, this morning I was teaching and I couldn't be at the board meeting, however I am happy to hear that the board approved a rat exclusion plan. You do have my permission to enter my condo. Unfortunately, I will be at work all day on Thursday, however both my downstairs and next door (Steve) neighbors have the key to my condo. I will check with them if they could be around. Thank you.

From: Stephen Steiner
    To: Donna Rickman
Subject: Re: RATS IN THE CEILINGS

NOVEMBER 28, 2022 / 11:50 PM

I will allow them to put in a trap door. As long as they are professionals who know what they are doing. I also want a phone number of one of the people collecting the traps. When I hear one go off I do not want to wait a few days for someone to come out to collect. There are a lot of new ones in my crawlspace. Every evening I hear them come up the pipes at the back patio area and run down the ceiling in my closet. Someone needs to check downstairs where the utility closet is located. That is where they are coming in.

And when this is all done is there a clean up crew to clean the crawlspace?

Thanks for getting this done and sorry for being so difficult. Hearing rats running around all night was making me go insane.

Hope you had a great Thanksgiving.

I am available on Thursday.

From: Stephen Steiner
    To: Giuseppe Vezzoli
Subject: Re: Board approved Rat Exclusion Plan

NOVEMBER 28, 2022 / 11:54 PM

I went ahead and approved them to come into my unit. If you give your key I will let them in unless Thomas is going to be there.

From: Donna Rickman
    To: Stephen Steiner
Subject: RE: RATS IN THE CEILINGS

NOVEMBER 29, 2022 / 9:24 AM

Thank you, Stephen. I will give you a contact number once I know who will be maintaining the traps.

A SPECIAL PLACE

From: Donna Rickman
To: Stephen Steiner
Subject: FW: RATS IN THE CEILINGS

NOVEMBER 30, 2022 / 6:17 PM

Are you available between 2:30 pm and 3:00 pm tomorrow for the trap door installation? By the way it might be sooner than 2:30 but they could only give me a rough estimate. Yes, you can request contact information so you can call for them to collect the traps during business hours. The utility closet was checked and closed according to Shane from Western Exterminators. I will double check tomorrow.

From: Donna Rickman
To: Stephen Steiner
Subject: FW: RATS IN THE CEILINGS

NOVEMBER 30, 2022 / 6:36 PM

I meant 4:00 pm for the installation. Thank you!

From: Stephen Steiner
To: Donna Rickman
Subject: Re: RATS IN THE CEILINGS

NOVEMBER 30, 2022 / 9:40 PM

4 pm is good.

2 (See p. 76)
SECOND HOLE /
FIRST ACCESS PANEL

BREAKER PANEL
SIMILAR TO ONE
PURCHASED
BY DONNA

MASSIVE
RODENT NEST
ABOVE DRYER

43

Mo	Tu	We	Th	Fr	Sa	Su
			~~1~~	~~2~~	~~3~~	~~4~~
~~5~~	~~6~~	~~7~~	~~8~~	~~9~~	~~10~~	~~11~~
~~12~~	~~13~~	~~14~~	~~15~~	~~16~~	~~17~~	~~18~~
~~19~~	~~20~~	~~21~~	~~22~~	~~23~~	~~24~~	~~25~~
~~26~~	~~27~~	~~28~~	~~29~~	~~30~~	~~31~~	

DECEMBER

171 DAYS UNRESOLVED

A SPECIAL PLACE

From: Donna Rickman   *DECEMBER 6, 2022 / 7:00 PM*
  To: Stephen Steiner
Subject: FW: RATS IN THE CEILINGS

I have your bulbs! I will be by tomorrow in the afternoon. If you are not home I will leave them on your doorstep.

From: Stephen Steiner   *DECEMBER 7, 2022 / 2:48 AM*
  To: Donna Rickman
Subject: Re: FW: RATS IN THE CEILINGS

Thanks, Donna, appreciate it!

These emails are unrelated to the rodent infestation and instead pertain to the volunteer work I performed for the HOA.

Earlier that year, based on "discussion" with neighbors, the HOA removed the sitting president, and appointed Shelley Westall as her replacement. Shortly thereafter, the management company, The Gaffney Group — which had been responsive and effective in maintaining the property — was abruptly replaced by Seabreeze Management. These changes were implemented quickly and without clear explanation.

During HOA meetings, it was proposed that we (the few Homeowners that attended the meetings) form the Palms Architecture and Landscaping Committee. The goal was for several homeowners, including myself, to walk the property and make aesthetic and functional improvement recommendations to the Board. At the time, the complex was undergoing repainting, and new landscaping was being considered to reduce water usage.

Given my background in the homebuilding industry, I volunteered to assist. I created detailed layouts with recommended paint colors and lighting fixture options for the property. I also provided designs for drought-tolerant landscaping to replace grass-heavy areas requiring excessive irrigation. This project required a significant time investment — from researching appropriate lighting to coordinating with a lighting supplier, who ultimately offered the HOA a generous discount through my efforts.

However, while contributing to this project, I was simultaneously dealing with worsening conditions from a rodent infestation in my unit. The contamination in the crawlspace above my ceiling led to severe air quality issues, causing me to lose sleep and suffer physical symptoms. Despite this, the HOA and Seabreeze Management failed to act with any urgency.

Because of the rodent issue and my involvement with the Architecture and Landscaping Committee I was notified the committee was no longer needed. None of the work I had submitted was acknowledged or incorporated. Instead, the HOA selected off-the-shelf lighting fixtures that did not reflect the design recommendations I had spent weeks developing. Additionally, I had purchased Edison-style bulbs to demonstrate how the new lighting could appear when installed — those bulbs were removed and taken by the installer during the final project execution. The email correspondence in question was simply related to my attempt to retrieve those bulbs and does not concern the infestation or related health and property issues.

I had graciously contributed my time and effort to assist the HOA with color exploration, lighting design, and landscaping enhancements— work intended to benefit the entire community. Unfortunately, these contributions were quickly dismissed, a decision reflective of Shelley and Donna's continued lack of professionalism and what appeared to be a deliberate effort to push me out of the complex.

Neither the HOA, the exterminators, nor Seabreeze Management took any action to address or eradicate the rodent infestation for the remainder of the month.

2 (i) (See p. 76)

THE PALMS PAINT COLORS & LIGHTING

A SPECIAL PLACE

LANDSCAPING

DESERTSCAPE

900 BUILDING (NORTH AND SOUTH AREAS)
North and South areas full desert scape. Continuation of what is behind the building. Full or partial desert scape behind building.

800 BUILDING
Full or partial desert scape behind building.

700 BUILDING
Full or partial desert scape behind building.

GREENBELT BETWEEN EAST SIDE BUILDINGS
Full or partial desert scape of area, especially around the trees where grass growth is sparse.

600 & 700 BUILDING (BETWEEN)
Grassy area.

WALKWAY DIAGONAL AREA BY POOL (BETWEEN)
Full desert scape with new step stones.

600 BUILDING (NORTH AREA)
Full or partial desert scape.

500 & 400 BUILDING (BETWEEN)
Paver's to grassy area with increased desert scape.

200 & 400 BUILDING (BETWEEN)
Full or partial desert scape.

300 BUILDING
Increase to full desert scape.

BEHIND 100, 200, & 400 BUILDINGS
Full or partial desert scape similar to east side.

GRASSY AREA BETWEEN 200 & 300 BUILDING
Leave as a grassy area?

TENNIS COURTS
Could use a replanting at some point. The court lines definitely need to be redone sooner that later.

2023

Mo	Tu	We	Th	Fr	Sa	Su
						1
2	3	4	5	6	7	8
9	10	11	12	13	14	15
16	17	18	19	20	21	22
23	24	25	26	27	28	29
30	31					

JANUARY

202 DAYS UNRESOLVED

A SPECIAL PLACE

From: Stephen Steiner
To: Donna Rickman
Subject: Rats and roof

The rat situation has gotten worse again. They are still getting into the crawlspace and making a lot of noise and damage. Last night was extremely windy and something broke loose on the roof and was rolling around above my condo. I am hoping it did not cause an opening. The crawlspace still needs to be cleaned because when the summer comes it will start smelling again. Please find a solution to this. It is a hazard to everyone in the 800 building. All it takes is one rat to chew through a wire and cause a fire.

From December 7, 2022, through the entire month of January, both the HOA and Seabreeze Management failed to take any action regarding the severe conditions in my unit. Despite numerous attempts to communicate, my emails were ignored by both Shelley Westall and Donna Rickman. Their ongoing lack of professionalism and failure to respond left me living in conditions that could only be described as uninhabitable — comparable to those often associated with slum housing.

Phone calls were equally ineffective, as they routinely went to voicemail without any return communication. In order to document their inaction and establish a clear record of their negligence, I made it a point to conduct all communication via email. This ensured there would be an accurate and traceable account of their failure to fulfill their responsibilities.

2 ⓘ (See p. 76)

	Mo	Tu	We	Th	Fr	Sa	Su
			~~1~~	~~2~~	~~3~~	~~4~~	~~5~~
	~~6~~	~~7~~	~~8~~	~~9~~	10	11	12
	13	14	15	16	17	~~18~~	19
	20	21	~~22~~	~~23~~	24	~~25~~	26
	27	~~28~~					

FEBRUARY

230 DAYS UNRESOLVED

From: Stephen Steiner
    To: Donna Rickman, Shelley Westall, Gary Fritzen
Subject: Rat Problem

FEBRUARY 8, 2023 / 1:08 AM

Giving you an update.

The rat problem is incredibly bad. The activity is worse than before. Last night I had the pleasure of hearing a large rat enter and attack a female rat and her babies. They proceeded to chase each other into the bathroom and kitchen crawlspace where they continued with the fighting. This went on for over 4 hours. My entire unit reeks of rat urine! This has to be resolved. If not, the HOA will pay for a rental property, utilities, and all moving costs until my unit is rat free and repaired (removing the ceiling and all insulation, sanitizing crawlspace and inside air ducts, replacing all carpeting, and repainting the entire unit). Living in this rat infested condo is not good for my health and had made my life miserable. I have been getting horrible headaches that never go away. It is decreasing the value of my property along with the other units in the 800 building.

I will not be paying any HOA dues or late fees until my unit is repaired. I should not have to live this way. It has been almost a year since I notified you about the rats and still no one can find the entry point? How is this possible?

This must be done before the summer. The heat will make it unbearable. I have been more that patient in this matter.

From: Donna Rickman
    To: Stephen Steiner, Shelley Westall, Gary Fritzen
Subject: RE: Rat Problem

FEBRUARY 8, 2023 / 2:10 PM

I requested a report from Western Exterminator that will include documentation of the days they serviced your unit. Nick should be calling you shortly to pick up the footage from the camera in the crawl space. After the footage is reviewed, the extermination team will develop a plan of action depending on what they find.

In response to the HOA and Board's continued skepticism about the severity of the rodent infestation, Western Exterminators installed a video camera in the crawlspace to obtain visual evidence and verify the extent of the problem. After their equipment was removed, I installed my own home security camera—featuring motion detection, sound tracking, and night vision—to maintain ongoing surveillance and documentation.

From: Donna Rickman
    To: Stephen Steiner
    Cc: Shelley Westall, Gary Fritzen
Subject: FW: Rat Problem

FEBRUARY 8, 2023 / 10:25 PM

I forgot to mention that after Western Exterminators review the footage of the crawl space and propose a new action plan for rat extermination that may displace you from your space, you shouldn't have to carry the burden of paying for accommodations.

From: Stephen Steiner
    To: Donna Rickman
    Cc: Shelley Westall, Gary Fritzen
Subject: Re: FW: Rat Problem

FEBRUARY 9, 2023 / 10:10 AM

Thank you.

My biggest concern is the cleanup. I need it to be completed. I am going to sell and I do not want this to be an issue. Hopefully, they will find where the rats are entering. My stress level is at max.

The footage I captured clearly confirmed the presence of significant rodent activity, along with the extensive damage and accumulation of waste they were causing within the crawlspace.

A SPECIAL PLACE

FEBRUARY 28, 2023 / 2:51 PM

From: Donna Rickman
To: Stephen Steiner
Subject: Rats in common area attic space in building 800

The board has thoughtfully considered next steps after your neighbor advised the HOA during the Annual meeting on Saturday, February 25, 2023, that you were reporting ongoing rodents' problems. The HOA has also considered the email and short video that you sent to Donna Rickman, The Palms Community Manager, and me, HOA Board member on February 27, 2023. The video and photo were stated as being taken by your personally installed devices and provided as evidence of rats in the common area attic space.

Immediately at start of business day Monday morning (February 27, 2023) Donna Rickman emailed Western Exterminator Operations Manager, Chad McChesney, to reinspect and arrange to treat the common area attic space in building 800 and your unit for ongoing conditions that are preventing or delaying eradication.

Chad wishes to personally inspect your unit and the areas you are reporting rodents. He would also like to review your camera placement to update their response. Western Exterminator has made several attempts to reach you for the re-inspection of your condo. The exterminator and the HOA cannot fully address your issue without a visual inspection of your unit and the common area attic space.

Out of an abundance of concern for residents, the board has taken immediate and extraordinary steps to treat and prevent rodent intrusion in the entire building and the complex. In addition to regular grounds treatment, the HOA has hired two exterminators specializing in rodent infestations, cut access points in ceilings for bait boxes and cameras, sealed any potential ingress areas, and blocked outdoor access points by removing foliage and mature trees. It is also important to note that Western Exterminator has reported there are no current indications of the presence of rats or that rat excrement is present in the living space of your unit.

At this time, you are the only resident reporting a current rodent problem. Therefore, your cooperation with the exterminators is mandatory to prevent potentially infesting neighboring units.

It is the board's desire that you provide access to your unit for an inspection by Western Exterminators by close of business Thursday, March 2, 2023. If you are unable to make your unit available in that time frame you must notify Donna Rickman by call or text or email by close of business March 1, 2023 with a date the unit will be available for inspection.

If you do not respond or miss any scheduled inspection, the board cannot proceed with further evaluation and will have no choice but to consider the issue resolved.

Donna's combative email (again most likely written by Shelley Westall) was a direct reaction to my decision to contact the City of Palm Springs Code Enforcement. Between February 9th and February 28th, no action had been taken to address the ongoing rodent infestation. Frustrated and desperate for a resolution, I reached out to Code Enforcement in the hopes that they could intervene. However, it quickly became evident that Shelley and Donna were displeased with their involvement.

The veiled threat that missing any scheduled inspections would result in the issue being considered resolved was absurd. For almost a yeas, I endured significant inconvenience, allowing exterminators into my home at all hours while being forced to live in a hazardous environment. I had done everything in my power to cooperate, yet I was the one suffering the consequences.

The reason I was the only homeowner consistently reporting the rodent activity is explained by several factors:

1. *My unit is located on the second floor, where the noise from the crawlspace was more audible due to the fact that it was above my head, while residents on the first floor were unlikely to hear any activity.*

2. *The owner of Unit 810 (Giuseppe) had been in Italy for the past year caring for his elderly parents; upon recently returning, his work schedule required him to work long hours, often returning home late at night when activity may not have been as noticeable.*

3. *The owner of Unit 806 did not reside in the unit, as it belonged to his parents who did not occupy at the time; following his father's passing, he was in the process of preparing the property for sale.*

The remaining units in the 800 building were either operated as Airbnb rentals or owned by seasonal residents ("snowbirds") who only occupied their units during the winter months.

Their frustration stemmed from the fact that the extermination company had installed a webcam in the crawlspace but failed to capture any footage. However, when I placed my own security camera in the same area, I recorded numerous rats actively moving through the crawlspace. Rather than acknowledging the undeniable evidence, Shelley and Donna sought to shift attention away from the Board and Seabreeze Management. Instead of accepting accountability, they attempted to deflect blame onto me, falsely accusing me of delaying the resolution to a crisis they had neglected for far too long.

During this period, the toll on my physical and mental health became severe. My shingles outbreaks intensified, and my mental state began to rapidly decline. In response, my physician prescribed Lamotrigine as a mood stabilizer to help manage the escalating stress and emotional instability. The persistent inaction by the HOA and management left me in a constant state of fear—terrified that continued exposure to the infestation would result in contracting a serious rodent-borne illness.

Mo	Tu	We	Th	Fr	Sa	Su
		1	2	3	4	5
6	7	8	9	10	11	12
13	14	15	16	17	18	19
20	21	22	23	24	25	26
27	28	29	30	31		

MARCH

261 DAYS
UNRESOLVED

A SPECIAL PLACE

MARCH 1, 2023 / 12:20 AM

From: Stephen Steiner
To: Donna Rickman, Shelley Westall
Bcc: Four homeowners in the 800 building were blind copied.
Subject: Re: Rats in common area attic space in building 800

Dear Donna and HOA Board of Directors,

I am happy to allow the exterminator into my property to inspect the rodent invasion. This has been done many times over the last year. Nick used to inspect Monday, Wednesday, and Friday for approximately two months. It slowly tapered off and stopped after the cam that he installed was removed for viewing. I'd like to point out that I never received any information about what was recorded. It is unbelievable, that my camera records rodents every day and the "specialist's" camera doesn't. I am curious to know what happened to that video. Did the HOA directors retain it?

I appreciate you having Chad McChesney come to reinspect and arrange to treat the "common area attic space" (not sure what that space is) of building 800 and my unit for ongoing conditions that are preventing or delaying eradication. I am not sure how this is preventing or delaying eradication. It is clear the eradication did not happen because most likely the rodents have an entranceway, therefore, the primary focus of the exterminator should be not only the remove the rodents in the attic but preventing them to get in there. Apparently, the board doesn't understand that this is the main issue. Are we sure the rodents are not entering from the roof? How can we identify the entryway or these pests?

In addition, Chad and others have repeatedly checked the utility closet, my unit, the neighbor's unit, the crawlspace, and the entire building with no results. I personally gave Chad a tour of the building so he could inspect every possible entry point. Apparently, he is missing the main entry point. Given that I am not an expert on rodents, and I've been paid diligently my HOA fee, I was hoping to receive much better treatment from the HOA Board of Directors and Seabreeze.

I fail to see the immediate and "extraordinary" steps to treat and prevent the rodent intrusion of the entire building and complex. It is evident that the board and the management don't have rodents crawling on their heads at night or above the kitchen ceiling. I do remember the former exterminator checked my unit monthly and he was very attentive to keeping me informed about the rodent situation. Something hasn't been done in the last two months.

I also fail to see how Western Exterminator has reported no current indication of the presence of rats. Perhaps this is because he has not checked my unit in over a month. If you would like, you are welcome to stay in my unit overnight so you too can enjoy the nightly activity of the rats and their young enjoying life above my head. Please extend this invitation to the rest of the HOA Board of Directors.

The fact that I am the only resident reporting the rodent problem should not be a factor in resolving this issue. The response from the HOA "Board of Directors", what are they directing is very unclear at this point, sounds like a passive-aggressive response that is directed at me personally. I have been living with this for almost a year. I reported to you back in July 2022. It is impressive how neither the board nor you have been in touch to ask about the issues.

I have been more cooperative and very patient over the last year. I have allowed all exterminators to come into my home to inspect the crawlspace, place traps, and video cameras and nothing has changed. Treating me as missing any scheduled inspections and considering the issue resolved should be enough to terminate the job of the HOA directors and your job. The board is considering the issue resolved if I don't respond in two business days. Where is their response? In 2 months? Do I need to wait for the next meeting to get this resolved? Perhaps, our president should reside in the complex, not in a different State.

I don't think the Board and you understand the stress this has caused in the last few months. Over the summer, I mentioned this multiple times there was a smell of dead animals in my condo, perhaps a rodent or more than one died there.

I really hope that this issue will be resolved sooner rather than later, and hopefully, sanitization followed by new insulation be put in place. As I recall from the CCRs everything above the ceiling is HOA's responsibility. It is not my responsibility if the so-called "experts" are not able to do their job.

A SPECIAL PLACE

From: Donna Rickman
  To: Stephen Steiner
  Cc: Shelley Westall
Subject: RE: Rats in common area attic space in building 800

Stephen: I understand that Western has provided you with an appointment schedule and your next appointment is 3/03/2023. We all look forward to eliminating the remaining rats in the common area attic.

From: Code Enforcement - City of Palm Springs
  To: Stephen Steiner
Subject: WorkOrder: 1018039

MARCH 7, 2023 / 3:53 PM

Hi, I have contacted both HOA and Community manager. I am awaiting their response regarding the efforts that have been made to rectify the problem. I was told they have had several exterminators out to the property and are doing proactive work to ensure this matter is taken care of and doesn't return. I will be contacting them again this week as well as the property owner of the unit.

From: Donna Rickman
  To: Stephen Steiner
Subject: Rats

MARCH 13, 2023 / 6:23 PM

Hi Stephen: Have you seen any improvement lately regarding the rat situation?

From: Stephen Steiner
  To: Donna Rickman
Subject: Re: Rats

MARCH 13, 2023 / 6:27 PM

Hi Donna, The trapped rats are running around and slowly dying off. I only heard one last night. Today there was nothing. When do you think the clean up will begin. The weather is getting warmer and the smell will be unbearable.

From: Donna Rickman
  To: Stephen Steiner
Subject: RE: Rats

MARCH 13, 2023 / 7:05 PM

Hi Stephen: That is good news. Once Western is 100% sure the rats are eradicated will do the cleanup. I will make sure that the Tech is scheduled to come out this week to check again. Thank you for the feedback.

From: Donna Rickman
  To: Stephen Steiner
Subject: Rodents

MARCH 24, 2023 / 4:19 PM

Hi Stephen: How is the Rodent situation going? I hope they are all gone. Thank you.

From: Stephen Steiner
  To: Donna Rickman
Subject: Re: Rodents

MARCH 25, 2023 / 8:52 AM

Unfortunately no. New ones have entered and are doing the same. I can tell when they are new because they are constantly digging in the same spot making their nest.

	Mo	Tu	We	Th	Fr	Sa	Su
						~~1~~	~~2~~
	~~3~~	~~4~~	~~5~~	~~6~~	~~7~~	~~8~~	~~9~~
	10	11	12	13	14	15	16
	17	18	19	20	21	22	23
	24	25	26	27	28	29	30

APRIL

291 DAYS
UNRESOLVED

A SPECIAL PLACE

From: Donna Rickman
To: Stephen Steiner
Subject: Rodents

APRIL 4, 2023 / 12:20 PM

Western Pest Control would like to place an access door inside the master bedroom closet to gain access to where you hear the noises coming from. Please let me know if you approve.

From: Stephen Steiner
To: Donna Rickman
Subject: Re: Rodents

APRIL 5, 2023 / 6:17 PM

I approve.

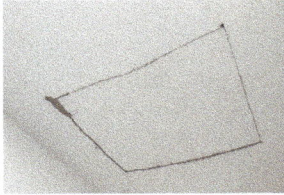

(See p. 76)

Western's regard for my property was minimal at best. Instead of properly installing an access panel, their technician used a drywall saw to cut a crude hole in the ceiling, then haphazardly attached a 2x4 to the center of the cut-out piece, leaving it to protrude slightly. That makeshift patch was presented as a "panel"—a clear sign of their lack of care and professionalism.

From: Donna Rickman
To: Stephen Steiner
Subject: RE: Rodents

APRIL 5, 2023 / 6:18 PM

Thank you.

From: Donna Rickman
To: Stephen Steiner
Subject: Rodents

APRIL 21, 2023 / 2:45 PM

I hope things are improving in your unit and you are doing well. Did Western install the access door in your master bedroom closet? Has the rat activity abated? Please let me know if there is something else you need.

From: Stephen Steiner
To: Donna Rickman
Subject: Re: Rodents

APRIL 22, 2023 / 1:03 AM

The rat situation got slightly better but they are still up there and they sound very large. I did hear from Western and they will be coming out to make holes in the ceiling to see what they need to do. I will keep you posted on the outcome.

From: Stephen Steiner
To: Code Enforcement - City of Palm Springs
Subject: Re: WorkOrder : 1018039

APRIL 26, 2023 / 8:12 AM

Since the last email, pretty much nothing has been done. The HOA and Seabreeze Management sent over another exterminator who went onto the roof and found a hole where I told him it would be a year ago. He plugged it up and said that it should be the end of the rats entering the crawlspace.

They also told me the cleanup would most likely be a new sanitizing spray that has recently been released and claims to eliminate all odor and bacteria and the urine soaked insulation did not require replacing. It has been over a year of rats making the crawlspace their home.

They also said the insulation that had fallen down was due the building settling and not the rats pulling it down to make a nest.

The email to Code Enforcement was the complete lack of response to my prior inquiries. Despite making numerous phone calls after receiving no replies to my emails, I eventually spoke with someone who informed me that the HOA had supposedly resolved the issue. However, no one from Code Enforcement ever contacted me via email or phone to provide this update. Had they done so, I would have been able to clarify that no action had actually been taken. Following that conversation, I was unable to receive any further responses from Code Enforcement, either by phone or email.

Once again, Shelley and Donna prolonged my suffering by allowing yet another month to pass without taking meaningful action—demonstrating a complete disregard for my health, well-being, and the seriousness of the situation.

Mo	Tu	We	Th	Fr	Sa	Su
1	2	3	4	5	6	7
8	9	10	11	12	13	14
15	16	17	18	19	20	21
22	23	24	25	26	27	28
29	30	31				

MAY

322 DAYS UNRESOLVED

A SPECIAL PLACE

From: Stephen Steiner
To: Donna Rickman
Subject: Airbnb

Please let the Airbnb units know the owners who live on the property do not enjoy hearing a bunch of college students throwing up and yelling at each other at this hour along with the screaming children in the pool during the day.

From: Donna Rickman
To: Stephen Steiner, Shelley Westall
Subject: RE: Airbnb

MAY 15, 2023 / 4:07 PM

Thank you for your email. I will send an email blast.

Under the management of Seabreeze and with Shelley Westall serving as President of the HOA, the number of units operating as short-term Airbnb rentals in the complex increased dramatically. This occurred despite the City of Palm Springs' ordinance limiting such rentals to no more than 20% of available housing. It was evident that neither Shelley nor Donna made any attempt to enforce this regulation. Additionally, the city requires a minimum 30-day stay for short-term rentals, yet many guests were staying for only a few days—often over long weekends—further highlighting the lack of oversight and compliance.

The complex quickly lost its residential integrity and began to resemble a revolving-door party destination, filled with loud, transient guests. My unit, located adjacent to the pool, was especially impacted by the constant disturbances, including unsupervised children and intoxicated visitors. This ongoing chaos only intensified the stress I was already under due to the unresolved rodent infestation.

Because of the HOA's incompetence and the repeated delays in addressing the infestation, coupled with the deterioration of my physical and mental health, I began seeking legal representation to help resolve the situation. My home had become uninhabitable, plagued by the overwhelming stench of decaying rodents, feces, urine, and the relentless noise of activity in the crawlspace above. What I didn't realize was how difficult it would be to find legal assistance—most attorneys refused to take on an HOA, as if these organizations operated with unchecked authority. As one attorney bluntly put it, "An HOA has more power than God." Eventually, Rhona Kauffman agreed to a consultation, which marked the beginning of yet another arduous and deeply frustrating chapter.

ENTER RHONA
EXIT DONNA

From: Rhona S. Kauffman
To: Stephen Steiner
Subject: Consultation

MAY 23, 2023 / 3:06 PM

This shall serve to confirm your consultation at my Palm Desert office for May 31, 2023 at 4 pm at my Palm Desert office addressed below. Please email if possible the governing documents prior to the meeting.

From: Rhona S. Kauffman
To: Stephen Steiner
Subject: RE: Consultation

MAY 29, 2023 / 2:29 PM

Good afternoon, I just left you a message. I have to change your appointment to 1 pm if you are available. Please confirm thank you.

From: Stephen Steiner
To: Rhona S. Kauffman
Subject: RE: Consultation

MAY 30, 2023 / 1:40 PM

Morning, Sorry for the late response. 1 pm works for me.

From: Giuseppe Vezzoli
To: Stephen Steiner
Subject: (No Subject)

MAY 31, 2023 / 9:14 PM

They are talking about rats.

These emails were exchanged during an HOA meeting held via Zoom. Since Giuseppe had recently returned from Italy, he was one of the few homeowners who regularly attended. The virtual format allowed participants to engage directly with one another, but unfortunately, overall attendance was consistently low. Out of 88 units in the complex, typically only about five homeowners took part in the meetings.

From: Stephen Steiner
To: Giuseppe Vezzoli
Subject: Re: (No Subject)

MAY 31, 2023 / 9:23 PM

Tell them that I left in anger that Donna can leave the job with no repercussions and I had to suffer and still suffer because of her lack of management.

She did not have to go through what I still am going through. My life was ruined and turned into a daily nightmare because of her. She ruined my home and life and just walks away.

Tell them. Tell them all how I had to go on medication because I went crazy and horrible shingles. She turned me into someone I did not want to become. And she gets to continue her charmed life. How wonderful for her!

During the HOA meeting, it was announced that Donna was being transferred to another property—likely a strategic move to shield Seabreeze Management from any potential legal repercussions. It was particularly unsettling to hear the Board commend her for the "excellent work" she had done while managing The Palms, despite the ongoing issues and mismanagement that had severely impacted my living conditions.

From: Stephen Steiner
To: Rhona S. Kauffman
Subject: Re: Consultation

MAY 31, 2023 / 9:27 PM

I asked Giuseppe if he had the Rat Exclusion Plan and it was not attached to his email either. Most likely BS.

There is a HOA meeting that started at 7 pm which I attended and left in anger after it was announced that Donna will no longer be managing this property.

So she messes up my life and then changes properties. I am beyond anger. I want to sue her personally. She ruined my life and defamed my character and all she had to do is change properties? Beyond angry.

A SPECIAL PLACE

From: Stephen Steiner
To: Giuseppe Vezzoli
Subject: Re: (No Subject)

MAY 31, 2023 / 9:30 PM

The fact that all she had to do is change properties to get out of being responsible for completely messing up my health and mind and well-being is beyond me. I will sue Seabreeze Management and Donna and Western Exterminators. They are all crooks.

From: Rhona S. Kauffman
To: Stephen Steiner
Subject: RE: Consultation

MAY 31, 2023 / 10:59 AM

See you at 10 am. Sorry for the confusion.

From: Stephen Steiner
To: Rhona S. Kauffman
Subject: Re: Consultation

MAY 31, 2023 / 11:19 AM

En Route.

3 **e** (See p. 76)

Mo	Tu	We	Th	Fr	Sa	Su
			~~1~~	~~2~~	~~3~~	~~4~~
~~5~~	~~6~~	~~7~~	~~8~~	~~9~~	10	~~11~~
12	~~13~~	14	~~15~~	~~16~~	~~17~~	~~18~~
~~19~~	20	~~21~~	22	23	~~24~~	~~25~~
~~26~~	~~27~~	~~28~~	~~29~~	30		

JUNE

352 DAYS UNRESOLVED

From: Rhona S. Kauffman
To: Stephen Steiner
Subject: Re: Consultation

JUNE 1, 2023 / 9:28 AM

I'm not sure why you're upset because this is a good thing she screwed up and now we have the opportunity to allow them to make it right.

Please let me know who the new property management company is or is it the same. And do you know the name of the new manager?

A little later today I will be sending you the retainer agreement. Have a nice morning.

From: Stephen Steiner
To: Rhona S. Kauffman
Subject: Re: Consultation

JUNE 1, 2023 / 12:56 PM

I should always look at the positive but my life in the last three years went from incredible to completely tragic and people very close to me turned their backs, took advantage, manipulated, and pretty much threw me away. I couldn't understand because I supported them mentally, financially, and never vanished.

So mentally I am damaged and when I was in the meeting (which are a joke because we have 88 units and only about 4 owners show up to the meeting), President of Board, was praising Donna. Hearing that was very painful and so not to look insane on camera I left the meeting. This is why I need you. Your brain works opposite of mine.

From: Stephen Steiner
To: Shelley Westall
Bcc: Giuseppe Vezzoli
Subject: CC&Rs and Rat Exclusion Plan

JUNE 1, 2023 / 4:23 PM

Do you have the most recent copy of the CC&Rs? The version I have is from the 80s. I also would like the Rat Exclusion Plan that Donna emailed Giuseppe but never attached the document. Thank You

---

From: Shelley Westall
To: Stephen Steiner
Cc: Donna Rickman, Paul Johnson
Subject: Re: CC&Rs and Rat Exclusion Plan

JUNE 1, 2023 / 8:32 PM

The latest version of the CCRs is from the 80s. The Board tried to update the document in 2016-2017 but it failed to get enough votes. I haven't seen a rat exclusion plan. I am adding Donna and Paul to this email so one of them can follow up. We have another exterminator starting Monday.

From: Stephen Steiner
To: Rhona S. Kauffman
Subject: The Palms - CC&Rs and Rat Exclusion Plan

JUNE 1, 2023 / 8:38 PM

Every email I send to you will start with The Palms so it will make it easier for you to search for all my emails related to this case. Here is the response I received from Shelley. Paul Johnson is replacing Donna.

From: Donna Rickman
To: Stephen Steiner, Shelley Westall
Cc: Paul Johnson
Subject: FW: Board approved Rat Exclusion Plan

JUNE 2, 2023 / 6:56 PM

I did attach the presentation to Giuseppe Vezzoli on November 28, 2022. Please see the email below.

From: Stephen Steiner   *JUNE 2, 2023 / 7:43 PM*
To: Donna Rickman
Subject: Re: Board approved Rat Exclusion Plan

Thank you, Donna.

From: Stephen Steiner   *JUNE 2, 2023 / 7:47 PM*
To: Rhona S. Kauffman
Subject: The Palms - Rodent Prevention and Control Plan

Here is the plan that completely failed.

From: Rhona S. Kauffman   *JUNE 2, 2023 / 8:19 PM*
To: Stephen Steiner
Subject: Re: The Palms - Rodent Prevention and Control Plan

No problem I can work with that. I'll move forward and prepare what we discussed.

From: Stephen Steiner   *JUNE 2, 2023 / 8:33 PM*
To: Rhona S. Kauffman
Subject: Re: The Palms - Rodent Prevention and Control Plan

Great. Shelley said they hired another exterminator company.

From: Rhona S. Kauffman   *JUNE 4, 2023 / 1:05 PM*
To: Stephen Steiner
Subject: RETAINER

PLEASE PRINT OUT AND REVIEW AND IF NO QUESTIONS INITIAL AT PARAGRAPH 11 AND THEN SIGN AND RETURN VIA EMAIL SCANNED. THIS AGREEMENT TAKEN FROM THE CALIFORNIA STATE BAR. HAVE A NICE REST OF THE WEEKEND.

From: Stephen Steiner   *JUNE 4, 2023 / 1:58 PM*
To: Rhona S. Kauffman
Subject: Re: RETAINER

Hope your weekend was relaxing.

I have attached the signed document. You mentioned mediation with both the HOA and Seabreeze. Is this something we have to do?

They treated me so poorly and made living at The Palms unbearable. I want them to pay for all of the emotional distress, shingles, defamation of character, and living in a toxic condo for a year. I don't think they know how many times I considered ending it all because the stress and depression compounded with the shingles made life extremely painful.

After the HOA meeting where they all were happy, laughing, and praising Donna, I don't want to hear their lies about fixing a problem they ignored. It will be another hole in my ceiling and nothing else. None of the Board members of Seabreeze Management would ever live the way I did.

A SPECIAL PLACE

From: Stephen Steiner
To: Rhona S. Kauffman
Subject: The Palms - I think I contracted F.tularensis

JUNE 12, 2023 / 7:26 PM

I just recovered from a horrible week of pain. I assumed that it was shingles but today I googled skin diseases that can be transmitted through inhaling rat feces and urine and what I have is more like F.tularensis. My shingles was never this bad so I believe I might have contracted F.tularensis. They swell and leave big holes in the skin.

Google F.tularensis and check out the images. I have photos of my back and chest with these and this past week I got one on my cheek, chin and stomach. I am going to go to my doctor tomorrow so they can take a look and hopefully test.

If it does come back positive for this virus the HOA and Seabreeze will pay for the suffering they cause me for an entire year and destroying my health.

I always wondered why I kept getting the sores even after I doubled my Valtrex dose for shingles.

From: Rhona S. Kauffman
To: Stephen Steiner
Subject: Re: The Palms - I think I contracted F.tularensis

JUNE 13, 2023 / 12:29 PM

I am so sorry you're going through this and I am working on your letter this week to the HOA. I will forward to you for your review first.

From: Rhona S. Kauffman
To: Stephen Steiner
Subject: Signed retainer for your files

JUNE 15, 2023 / 2:07 PM

[Attached: Signed retainer]

From: Donna Rickman
To: Stephen Steiner
Subject: THE PALMS HOA - INTRODUCTION OF NEW GENERAL MANAGER

JUNE 21, 2023 / 5:12 PM

Dear Members:

Please click here to read the letter of introduction from Paul Johnson, the new General Manager of The Palms Homeowners Association. Paul has over twenty-eight years of experience in the industry that will benefit the Association when working with the Board of Directors and residents.

From: Scott Fisher
To: Stephen Steiner
Subject: Responding To Your Recent Contact

JUNE 23, 2023 / 5:58 PM

I hope that this finds you well. It seems that I owe you an apology for not responding to your inquiry about the HOA issues sooner. I now understand that you initiated the contact through my website at a particular time when my marketing reps. were revamping and updating my website.

Nevertheless, I will investigate why I was unable to see your inquiry earlier. In any event, I am truly sorry that I did not respond to your contact sooner. Jeff told me that you have retained a local attorney to assist you with your HOA dispute. I hope that it works out for you. Jeff also advised me that you had also reached out to me by phone and left messages on several occasions about this matter.

I scoured my telephone records, and I have no record of any calls or voicemail messages from you. It would assist me to learn whether you also made calls to my office or left voicemail messages for me, in addition to your inquiry through my website. Please let me know at your earliest opportunity.

I was introduced to attorney Scott Fisher through my partner in the late 1990s. Based in Los Angeles, Scott's legal expertise primarily focused on real estate matters, and while not specific to HOA law, I reached out to him early on in hopes of obtaining a referral to someone more suited to the situation I was facing.

From: Stephen Steiner
To: Scott Fisher
Subject: Re: Responding To Your Recent Contact

JUNE 23, 2023 / 6:12 PM

No worries. I left a message from the number on your website. To this day they have not done anything to resolve the issue. I literally went crazy and now everyone is scared to be around me. Life got hard and depressing. How have you been?

From: Scott Fisher
To: Stephen Steiner
Subject: Re: Responding To Your Recent Contact

JUNE 23, 2023 / 6:15 PM

I'm doing fine, mainly focused on work but looking forward to some downtime this weekend. I hope that your attorney can get some relief for you. Please feel free to keep me posted.

From: Stephen Steiner
To: Scott Fisher
Subject: Re: Responding To Your Recent Contact

JUNE 23, 2023 / 6:16 PM

I hope so too. I want them to pay for what they did. They had the nerve to accuse me of contributing to the rat infestation. Nuts!!

From: Rhona S. Kauffman
To: Stephen Steiner
Subject: RE: The Palms - I think I contracted F.tularensis

JUNE 30, 2023 / 8:11 PM

HOW IS YOUR HEALTH???? IT IS IMPORTANT AND COMES FIRST... I AM PREPARING AS WE DISCUSSED BUT I WAS WAITING TO HEAR FROM YOU. CAN WE SPEAK ON MONDAY?

I found this email both confusing and frustrating. The vague statement—"Hear from me?"—left me unsure of her intentions. What exactly was she waiting to hear from me about? The message offered no meaningful communication, no direction, and certainly no sense of urgency. At the time, I was seriously ill, suffering from a painful fungal infection—one of the conditions specifically outlined in the Rat Exclusion Plan—which had spread across my hand and back. This was further compounded by a severe shingles outbreak, brought on by the prolonged stress and unrelenting conditions in my home.

During our initial consultation, Rhona had stated she would draft a demand letter and initiate mediation proceedings. I was hesitant about pursuing mediation, as Shelley and Donna had shown no willingness to address the rodent infestation or clean up the contamination. Nevertheless, Rhona assured me that California law required mediation prior to filing a lawsuit. Trusting her legal expertise, I reluctantly agreed, despite strong concerns that this would only grant the HOA more time to continue neglecting the situation.

Only later did I learn that mediation is not legally required in such cases under California law. This revelation was both shocking and deeply troubling. To make matters worse, Rhona became increasingly difficult to contact—failing to respond to emails, ignoring phone calls, and offering no consistent communication. At the time, I rationalized her inaccessibility as the result of a demanding schedule. In hindsight, my decision not to question her lack of responsiveness was a costly mistake.

From: Stephen Steiner
To: Rhona S. Kauffman
Subject: RE: The Palms - I think I contracted F.tularensis

JUNE 30, 2023 / 11:23 PM

I am feeling a little better. Monday is good for me. Rats have returned. Have a great weekend.

3 2 (See p. 76)

Mo	Tu	We	Th	Fr	Sa	Su
					~~1~~	~~2~~
~~3~~	~~4~~	~~5~~	~~6~~	~~7~~	~~8~~	~~9~~
10	~~11~~	12	~~13~~	14	15	16
17	~~18~~	~~19~~	20	21	~~22~~	23
24	~~25~~	~~26~~	~~27~~	28	~~29~~	30
~~31~~						

JULY

383 DAYS
UNRESOLVED

A SPECIAL PLACE

From: Stephen Steiner   *JULY 3, 2023 / 9:53 AM*
    To: Rhona S. Kauffman
Subject: RE: The Palms - I think I contracted F.tularensis

Let me know what time you would like to talk. I want to sue the HOA, Shelley, Donna, and Seabreeze Management. I do not want mediation. They don't deserve it and I want them to pay for the suffering, horrible case of shingles, mental anguish, massive depression, damage to the condo and damage to my character. It was all their fault and they know it.

They made me suicidal so my doctor put me on Lamotrigine. It helped a little but the issue is still going on.

FIRST, they WILL repair my condo! The contents of my condo will be packed and put into storage. The ceiling will be removed throughout the entire condo, all insulation will be removed, all electrical will be checked and repaired, HVAC completely replaced since the rats got into the main unit, everything sanitized, new insulation installed, new drywall installed, new carpeting, new paint, new kitchen, new bathrooms, EVERYTHING!

They put me through HELL. Everyone in the complex witnessed my suffering. My property value has decreased more than the other units. They treated me like trash. I did not deserve any of this. Even the exterminators said I should not be living in this toxic condo. The last year was brutal and they need to pay for what they did which was nothing.

Let me know what a good time is for you to discuss. I want to end the constant noise of rats and stench they leave behind.

From: Stephen Steiner   *JULY 9, 2023 / 4:11 PM*
    To: Rhona S. Kauffman
Subject: Update

Checking in on progress. I would like to get the condo repaired as soon as I can so I can sell it. The complex has become an Airbnb complex. I know for a fact that most of the Airbnb are illegal. Palm Springs put a cap on Airbnb rentals and there is a $5,000 fine for those who did not register with the city. Isn't the management company supposed to monitor this?

From: Stephen Steiner   *JULY 22, 2023 / 2:03 AM*
    To: Rhona S. Kauffman
Subject: Re: The Palms - Checking in

Checking to see if you sent the draft. I am hoping to get this resolved and condo fixed so I can sell and move away from this Airbnb complex. Have a great weekend.

From: Rhona S. Kauffman   *JULY 25, 2023 / 8:46 AM*
    To: Stephen Steiner
Subject: Re: The Palms - Checking in

Good morning, yes, absolutely I have a draft letter which I will forward to you in the next few days

The next few days? What have you been doing since May 23rd till now?

Rhona made no meaningful progress on my case. Instead, she mirrored the same pattern of delay and avoidance exhibited by the HOA and Seabreeze Management. In hindsight, I should have terminated her representation much earlier, as her inaction only served to prolong an already unbearable situation.

Rhona's failure to act was especially troubling given the circumstances. Shelley was well aware that, due to her own lack of urgency and poor decision-making, the cost of repairs had escalated significantly—costs that would ultimately fall on the HOA, as the crawlspace is their responsibility. One would expect any competent attorney to immediately pursue legal action against both the HOA and Seabreeze Management under such clear liability. Instead, Rhona did nothing. It was becoming increasingly clear that something was not right— there appeared to be a deeper, possibly underhanded dynamic at play.

Mo	Tu	We	Th	Fr	Sa	Su
1	2	3	4	5	6
7	8	9	10	11	12	13
14	15	16	17	18	19	20
21	22	23	24	25	26	27
28	29	30	31

AUGUST

414 DAYS
UNRESOLVED

A SPECIAL PLACE

From: Stephen Steiner
  To: Rhona S. Kauffman
Subject: The Palms

AUGUST 2, 2023 / 7:39 PM

A friend just called me and said that a complex in Palm Desert has a rat problem and they are filing a lawsuit against the HOA. Guess I'm not alone. Any progress on my lawsuit. I am hoping the new project manager and the HOA rewrite the CCRs to add the crawlspace to become the homeowners responsibility. Let me know as soon as possible if you get the letter to them. I don't want them to think the rat problem is considered resolved since there has been no communication between me and them.

From: Rhona S. Kauffman
  To: Stephen Steiner
Subject: Re: The Palms

AUGUST 2, 2023 / 8:01 PM

Yes, I would like to meet with you next Wednesday. I have a draft letter I've been working on. Are you available next Wednesday to meet with me at my Palm Desert office? Please advise.

Rhona's repeated requests for in-person meetings quickly became unreasonable. From the moment I retained her as counsel, she never once visited my condo to witness the conditions I was living in—conditions that were central to my case. Despite this, she consistently insisted that I travel to her office, which was located 40 minutes away. Each time I complied, our meetings were held in an outdated conference room because her office was perpetually under renovation.

What made this even more frustrating was that everything we discussed could have been easily handled over the phone or via email. Her insistence on in-person meetings seemed unnecessary and, in hindsight, appeared to serve no purpose other than to delay progress. Each visit added time and stress while producing no meaningful results.

From: Stephen Steiner
  To: Rhona S. Kauffman
Subject: Re: The Palms

AUGUST 3, 2023 / 10:58 AM

I can. If it is easier for you we can Zoom. Let me know what time.

From: Rhona S. Kauffman
  To: Stephen Steiner
Subject: RE: The Palms

AUGUST 4, 2023 / 7:29 PM

I can meet you at 12:30 pm at my Palm Desert office on Wednesday. Is that acceptable to you?

Please advise.

From: Stephen Steiner
  To: Rhona S. Kauffman
Subject: Re: The Palms

AUGUST 5, 2023 / 1:47 AM

See you then.

From: Rhona S. Kauffman
  To: Stephen Steiner
Subject: Re: The Palms

AUGUST 5, 2023 / 8:28 AM

Great.

A SPECIAL PLACE

From: Rhona S. Kauffman
To: Stephen Steiner
Subject: Tomorrow

AUGUST 9, 2023 / 1:43 AM

Stephen, I have been sick with a stomach virus for a couple of days that went around my office. I am going in tomorrow to pick up documents and give clients some documents. I thought we would postpone but only a few days. You had suggested on the telephone and what I would like to do is email you the draft letter by no later than Monday and then set up a conference call on Tuesday with you to review. Also, I need a current status of your health and the reports. Please let me know you receive this email. Sorry for how late it is but I am still up and was concerned about meeting tomorrow with the stomach virus.

Yet another unnecessary delay. This time, she claimed she had contracted a stomach flu that was "circulating through her office." The statement raised immediate doubts — she didn't have a traditional office staff. Each time I visited, I checked in with the building's front desk, but I never actually stepped foot into her office. I was always told it was "under renovation," and our meetings were held in a shared conference room used by various tenants — the kind of space rented by the hour in coworking facilities.

There were no visible employees, no signage, and no indication of an active legal office. It began to feel like the entire setup was designed to create the illusion of a professional operation. In reality, she appeared to be working alone, and for all I know, the office space may have been used solely for appearances — or simply as a mailing address.

From: Stephen Steiner
To: Rhona S. Kauffman
Subject: Re:Tomorrow

AUGUST 9, 2023 / 9:54 AM

Sorry about the stomach virus, I've gotten them and they are not fun. My health is okay for now. There are no reports other than an email to my doctor in LA telling him I was going insane and all the tenants witnessing my mental decline. The emails I supplied to you show my downward slide into insanity. All my neighbors can testify how it drove me to a mental breakdown. My doctor added bipolar medication to help with the stress.

I want to sue for the complete removal and replacement of the entire ceiling and insulation including sanitizing all of it. The entire air conditioning system needs to be replaced. The rats fell into the closet where it is located. I had to repair it a few months back because one of the sensors was broken most likely from a rat. Several have fallen onto it and climbed their way out through the hole that still is there.

In the images I supplied there are some from my thermal camera. I purchased one to see where the rats were living. It shows where all the rat nests are located and there are a lot of them. The kitchen has the largest amounts. Actually, the entire condo is blanketed with nests. You have the video footage and if you need more I have a ton.

For the HOA and Seabreeze management to put me through over a year of torture, I want them to understand the suffering I endured and continue to endure. I was disrespected and made to feel insignificant. I was understanding and patient with them. I worked with their schedule. Numerous exterminators entered my condo 3 times a week. Three entry holes were cut into my ceiling (which they are supposed to seal up), set traps that basically did nothing. In return, they accused and threatened me. Instead of solving the problem, the HOA and Seabreeze would drag the problem out by making a new entry point and setting more traps. Even one of the exterminators was surprised I was still living in "this toxic environment".

The amount of rat urine and feces is incomprehensible. This summer has been brutal and the smell unbearable. I wish I could force Donna to live in my condo and enjoy inhaling the toxic air. They will pay for the entire repair of my condo. I notified them on day one about a rat in the crawlspace. No one should have to go through what I did. I am a complete mental case and my personal character was destroyed because of their incompetence. If they come back with "We were and still are working on the situation", I want you to add $1M to the lawsuit. They have no right to say that. If they were, there would be an exterminator here every day until there were no rats.

I haven't heard a peep from them in months. No calls, no emails, nothing. That is the respect I get from them. Please look into the lawsuit the Palm Desert complex filed against the HOA. I would like to know how similar it is and if Seabreeze is the management company. Most likely it is since they are based out there. We can do mediation. Here is how it will go. If I don't hear "Complete remodel" and "pain and suffering" it will go to court and will be a huge lawsuit. There is an enormous amount of evidence and an incredible amount of witnesses.

I did nothing wrong. They did and they will pay. They ruined my life and destroyed my home.

A SPECIAL PLACE

I am including a floor plan of the condo on page 76 to provide context for the thermal images, which were taken to document the location and extent of rodent contamination relative to the layout of the unit. The images clearly identify areas saturated with rodent urine and heavily impacted by fecal accumulation. Utilizing my thermal imaging device, I recorded comprehensive footage throughout the condo to visually capture the full scale of contamination and damage.

In these images, the blackened areas represent insulation that has been thoroughly soaked with rodent urine. In several shots, you can visibly track the path of urine as it traveled down the inside of the drywall—evidence of prolonged, unchecked nesting activity. The rodents established at least three major nests:

1. The first nest was situated above the HVAC unit, directly where the ductwork branches off to heat and cool both sides of the condo. This location offered the rats ideal conditions year-round—cool in summer, warm in winter.

2. The second nest was built above the light fixture and dryer in the laundry closet. This area provided consistent warmth from both the fixture and the dryer, making it a suitable and undisturbed nesting site.

3. The third and most active nest was located above the kitchen, directly above the cabinets and refrigerator. This nest utilized the ductwork running into the living and dining rooms. Since I primarily used the second bedroom/office, I had closed the kitchen and dining room vents to redirect airflow to the living area. This unintentionally funneled more heat and air conditioning through the ducts near the nest, allowing the rodents a stable, climate-controlled environment.

I submitted all of this documentation to Rhona as critical evidence. Yet, it appears that the material was either deliberately withheld or entirely disregarded by the HOA. Given the severity of what these images revealed—and the substantial remediation costs they implied—it is not unreasonable to believe this evidence was intentionally buried. The infestation was far more serious than the HOA, Seabreeze Management, or their counsel were willing to admit, and this thermal data proved it beyond dispute.

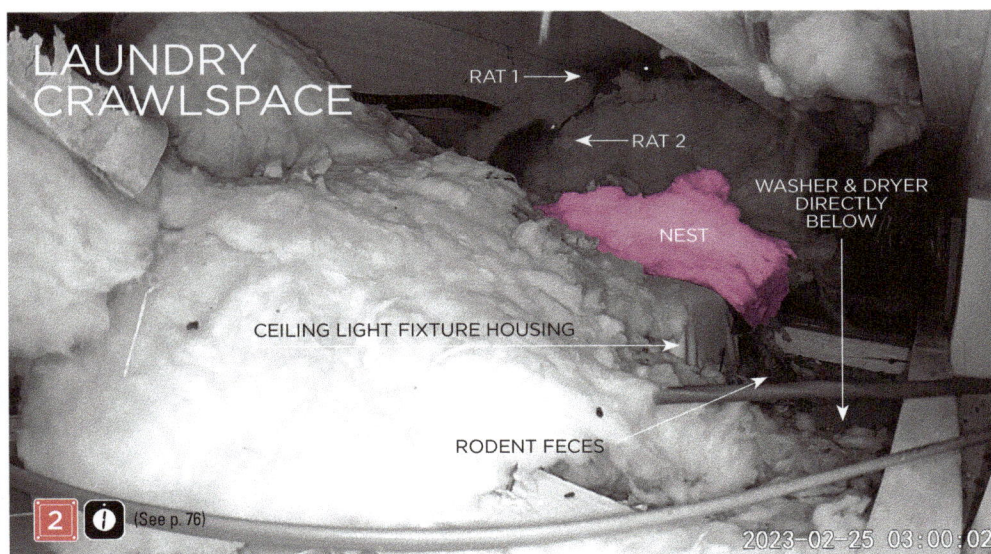

Rodents had torn down the insulation from the roof line to create a pass-through between both sides of the condo. One major nest was built directly above the dryer, next to the ceiling light fixture—a warm, concealed location that allowed them to thrive.

After the access panel was installed, Western Exterminators assigned technician Nick Valek to monitor the traps in this area three times a week—Monday, Wednesday, and Friday at 8:00 AM. This rigid schedule served no real purpose other than to increase my stress. I was home all day and would have known immediately if a trap had been triggered. But instead of waiting for my call, Nick came regularly, each time witnessing how much worse my physical and mental health was becoming.

After about two months, Nick told me he had found a new job. I could tell he was disturbed by what he had seen and didn't want to be part of what they were doing to me. He returned two days later with his manager, Chad McChesney, to show him the process until a replacement could be found.

During their visit, I explained that all the insulation in the crawlspace needed to be removed and replaced, as it was soaked with urine and feces. Chad responded that a sanitization spray—claiming to kill 99% of bacteria and viruses—would be sufficient. I objected, noting that dried droppings would eventually become airborne and enter the condo. I also pointed out that the insulation had been pulled down by the rodents and needed to be restored to its original position. Chad asked when the condo was built. When I said "1978," he replied, "That's why it looks like this. After 40 years, the building has settled and the insulation naturally fell." I looked at Nick, who rolled his eyes. He knew it was complete nonsense—just another excuse to avoid covering the cost of proper repair.

That was the end of the three-day trap checks. I never heard back from Western Exterminators.

A SPECIAL PLACE

CONDO FLOOR PLAN

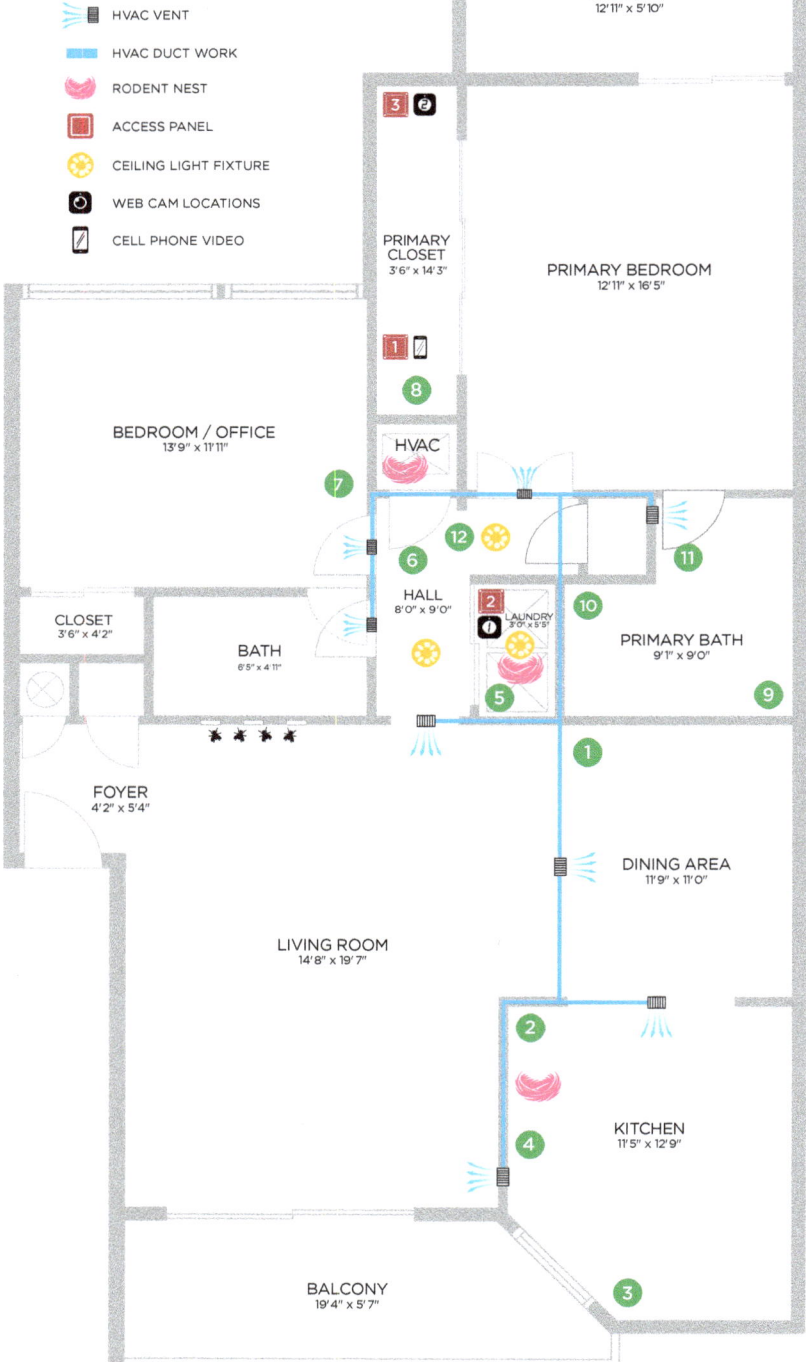

≫▤	HVAC VENT
▬	HVAC DUCT WORK
🩷	RODENT NEST
▥	ACCESS PANEL
⬤	CEILING LIGHT FIXTURE
◉	WEB CAM LOCATIONS
▯	CELL PHONE VIDEO

BALCONY
12'11" x 5'10"

3 ◉

PRIMARY CLOSET
3'6" x 14'3"

PRIMARY BEDROOM
12'11" x 16'5"

1 ▯

8

BEDROOM / OFFICE
13'9" x 11'11"

HVAC

7

6

12 ⬤

11

CLOSET
3'6" x 4'2"

BATH
6'5" x 4'11"

HALL
8'0" x 9'0"

2
LAUNDRY
3'0" x 5'5"

10

PRIMARY BATH
9'1" x 9'0"

⬤

5

9

1

FOYER
4'2" x 5'4"

DINING AREA
11'9" x 11'0"

LIVING ROOM
14'8" x 19'7"

2

KITCHEN
11'5" x 12'9"

4

BALCONY
19'4" x 5'7"

3

A SPECIAL PLACE

79.3°F   e=0.98
79.3°F
20240607-095939
MAX:82.4°F MIN:78.6°F 09:59AM

80.4°F   e=0.95
80.4°F
20240607-100249
MAX:88.8°F MIN:75.9°F 10:02AM

89.7°F   e=0.98
89.7°F
20240607-182830

84.9°F   e=0.98
84.9°F
20240607-182730

87.6°F   e=0.98
87.6°F
20240607-182526

88.1°F   e=0.98
88.1°F
20240607-182444

87.9°F   e=0.98
87.9°F
20240607-182447

79.1°F   e=0.98
79.1°F
20240607-095146
MAX:83.1°F MIN:78.8°F 09:51AM

80.9°F   e=0.95
80.9°F
20240607-100217
MAX:87.0°F MIN:77.9°F 10:02AM

91.7°F   e=0.85
91.7°F
20240607-181825

90.8°F   e=0.85
90.8°F
20240607-181759

80.9°F   e=0.95
80.9°F
20240607-100343
MAX:84.2°F MIN:78.6°F 10:03AM

From: Shonna Obeso
To: Stephen Steiner
Cc: Paul Johnson
Subject: Unit# 808

AUGUST 9, 2023 / 4:58 PM

Hello Mr. Steiner, I left you a voicemail message in addition to this email. I wanted to follow up and make sure everything has been resolved regarding the rodent treatments that were done. Please reply and let me know so I can forward all information to the General Manager.

From: Stephen Steiner
To: Rhona S. Kauffman
Subject: The Palms - Letter Regarding Rat Problem

AUGUST 9, 2023 / 6:50 PM

I received a voicemail and email from Seabreeze regarding the rat problem. From the email they sent they are under the impression that it is over and there is no cleanup.

Can you please let them know you are my attorney and that I hired you to represent me?

If they come back with "We will have another exterminator come out and make another hole and set traps", tell them I have endured over a year of people coming in and setting traps and it has accomplished nothing.

I have been more than patient with the entire situation and moving Donna to another property does not give them the right to start over with a clean slate. I am sick and tired of people walking all over me.

Please let them know they will be receiving your letter.

Please notify them today if you can. I don't want them to think they are done with this. If you want I can let them know they will be receiving your letter.

From: Stephen Steiner
To: Shonna Obeso
Bcc: Rhona S. Kauffman
Subject: Re: Unit# 808

AUGUST 10, 2023 / 8:15 PM

Not a single thing has been resolved regarding the rodent treatments. I continue to have a rat infestation. My entire crawlspace is littered with rat droppings and urine and only the summer temperatures have kept the rodent activity low. I will not get into the smell I have had to endure this summer.

Please refer back to the HOA, Donna, and the numerous exterminators that have made 3 entry points in my ceiling (which are supposed to be sealed up) and all the video footage that I recorded of the damage to my condo which by CC&Rs is the HOAs responsibility to repair.

Until my condo is completely free of rat urine, feces, and the rodents I will not consider this resolved. The new General Manager is aware of this situation.

From: Rhona S. Kauffman
To: Stephen Steiner
Subject: RE: Unit# 808

AUGUST 10, 2023 / 8:24 PM PM

Thank you, and the new general manager should have been aware from the beginning? I have your file and am working on it.

A SPECIAL PLACE

From: Rhona S. Kauffman
  To: Shonna Obeso
  Cc: Stephen Steiner
Subject: Stephen Steiner

Please be advised that Mr. Steiner retained my services a few weeks ago in regard to this serious and horrendous situation with the rodent infestation in his ceiling above his unit.

This has led to serious property damage and severe emotional distress suffered by Mr. Steiner due to the delays of the HOA in rectifying this problem.

I am currently reviewing the documents and I would respectfully request that you direct me to the Attorneys for the HOA for communication and service of correspondence in this regard. Thanking you in advance. Sincerely, Rhona S. Kauffman, Esq.

From: Shonna Obeso
  To: Stephen Steiner
  Cc: Paul Johnson
Subject: RE: Unit# 808

AUGUST 11, 2023 / 10:15 AM

Hi Steve, I am so sorry to hear. I have forwarded your response to the General Manager, as he is also CC'd on this email. Please ensure to "reply all" when corresponding so we may all be in the loop.

From: Rhona S. Kauffman
  To: Stephen Steiner
Subject: QUESTIONS

AUGUST 13, 2023 / 3:38 PM

Good afternoon, I am reviewing your emails and you say in 7/14/2022 email that you informed the HOA one year earlier in 7/2021. What happened, are there emails and did you wait a year until 7/2023 because it subsided? Please advise.

From: Stephen Steiner
  To: Rhona S. Kauffman
Subject: Re: QUESTIONS

AUGUST 13, 2023 / 4:53 PM

Hi, That was the month the previous management company (Gaffney Group) was terminated and Seabreeze Management was hired. It was never addressed.
I do remember speaking to Donna at that time about it. Since I worked in the homebuilder industry Donna set up a committee for the new paint job and landscaping. That was around the time I mentioned it to her. She told me it was probably a bird on the roof or a cat. It was the summer and the heat kept them away so I didn't pursue it. I went to Dallas at the end of December 2021 for 6 months to help my dad out and returned June 1, 2022. That was when the rats were out of control. I emailed Donna shortly after. That was the start of this mess. Let me know if you need any other info.

From: Rhona S. Kauffman
  To: Stephen Steiner
Subject: RE: QUESTIONS

AUGUST 13, 2023 / 4:58 PM

Please explain in that year from July 2021 to July 2022 what you did and what happened or did it go away and come back in July 2022 with a vengeance. I have read all the emails and it is horrendous what they have done. And you never received any formal letters from the board, correct?

From: Rhona S. Kauffman
To: Stephen Steiner
Subject: Re: QUESTIONS

Sounds good. You will have my letter draft tomorrow for sure as promised and then once you approve or tell me any changes, I will serve tomorrow. I have to confirm who your attorneys for the HOA are. Please email Donna now and ask her who the attorneys are for the HOA if you don't know already and if you do know then email me the name thank you.

From: Stephen Steiner
To: Rhona S. Kauffman
Subject: RE: QUESTIONS

I went to Istanbul at the end of June and returned in August. I honestly didn't think anything of the rat problem at the time. I figured it was a tiny mouse and was a random event. I sent the email to Donna when the rats kept digging in one corner of the bathroom crawlspace for several days. At that time I did not know how large the rats were. Over the next few weeks it became a big problem. I never received anything from the Board or Seabreeze. Eventually, Donna came over to discuss having a hole made in the crawlspace to have access. I did not want that and insisted they make one on the roof. She would not allow it because it would void the warranty. She could have contacted the roofing company to see if there was a way to have on installed without voiding the warranty. I was left to endure the numerous amount of exterminators in my unit and the three holes that they still need to seal up. I don't recall a single time when Donna or Shelley contacted me to see how I was doing. They did send me that nasty email after I got the city involved.

From: Stephen Steiner
To: Rhona S. Kauffman
Subject: RE: QUESTIONS

That was the month the previous management company (Gaffney Group) was terminated and Seabreeze Management was hired. It was never addressed. I do remember speaking to Donna at that time about it. Since I worked in the homebuilder industry Donna set up a committee for the new paint job and landscaping. That was around the time I mentioned it to her. She told me it was probably a bird on the roof or a cat. It was the summer and the heat kept them away so I didn't pursue it. I went to Dallas at the end of December 2021 for 6 months to help my dad out and returned June 1, 2022. That was when the rats were out of control. I emailed Donna shortly after. That was the start of this mess.

From: Stephen Steiner
To: Rhona S. Kauffman
Subject: Re: QUESTIONS

I will see if Donna responds to my email. I will send an email to Shelley as well. I have a feeling there is no attorney for this complex just like there are no real cameras on the property.

From: Stephen Steiner
To: Donna Rickman, Shelley Westall
Bcc: Rhona S. Kauffman
Subject: HOA Attorneys

Can you please email me the names of the attorneys for The Palms HOA?

From: Donna Rickman
To: Stephen Steiner
Cc: Paul Johnson
Subject: Manager

I haven't been the Manager since May 2023. Paul Johnson is the Manager and is copied on this email.

From: Rhona S. Kauffman
  To: Stephen Steiner
Subject: Question

AUGUST 14, 2023 / 8:49 PM

Did you ever get a copy of that plan to eradicate rats sent to G?

From: Stephen Steiner
  To: Rhona S. Kauffman
Subject: Re: Question

AUGUST 14, 2023 / 9:45 PM

I think I did. I remember it was a PDF explaining what basically is their job. I might have sent it to you. Let me check.

From: Stephen Steiner
  To: Rhona S. Kauffman
Subject: RE: The Palms - CC&Rs and Rat Exclusion Plan

AUGUST 14, 2023 / 9:51 PM

It was sent on June 1, 2023. I was preparing the file for you and you wanted the latest. Apparently they never revised it when they were supposed to. That explained the hand-typed CCRs.

From: Stephen Steiner
  To: Rhona S. Kauffman
Subject: Re: The Palms - CC&Rs and Rat Exclusion Plan

AUGUST 14, 2023 / 9:58 PM

Found the Rat Exclusion Plan. It even states that it is a health hazard. Why did they let this go on for so long? Apparently, the HOA didn't read it!

From: Stephen Steiner
  To: Paul Johnson
 Bcc: Rhona S. Kauffman
Subject: Attorneys for HOA

AUGUST 14, 2023 / 11:29 AM

Can I have the name or names of the attorneys for the HOA at the Palms?

From: Paul Johnson
  To: Stephen Steiner
Subject: RE: Attorneys for HOA

AUGUST 14, 2023 / 12:06 PM

Steve, per your attorney's request we have forwarded your attorney's information to The Palms Attorney (Guralnick & Gilliland, LLP) on Friday.

From: Stephen Steiner
  To: Paul Johnson
Subject: Re: Attorneys for HOA

AUGUST 14, 2023 / 12:08 PM

Thank you, Paul. Appreciate the quick response.

From: Stephen Steiner
  To: Rhona S. Kauffman
Subject: Update

AUGUST 14, 2023 / 12:29 PM

Last night the rats returned. I guess they knew we were talking about them. There was one that traveled through the entire ceiling checking to make sure what they left was still there. It started around 3am. Oddly, there were two owls cooing back and forth. I think they were waiting for him to exit and snatch him up.

From: Stephen Steiner
To: Rhona S. Kauffman
Subject: The Palms - Confirmation

AUGUST 14, 2023 / 12:38 AM

Wanted to make sure you received the Rat "Exclusion" and the attorneys names. Attaching both just in case.

From: Rhona S. Kauffman
To: Stephen Steiner
Subject: RE: The Palms - CC&Rs and Rat Exclusion Plan

AUGUST 20, 2023 / 6:48 PM

WHY IS THERE NOT A DATE ON THAT PLAN? IS THAT THE SAME PLAN THAT WAS ATTACHED TO THE EMAIL FROM DONNA TO YOUR NEIGHBOR ON November 28, 2023?

From: Rhona S. Kauffman
To: Stephen Steiner
Subject: RE: The Palms - CC&Rs and Rat Exclusion Plan

AUGUST 20, 2023 / 6:53 PM

And was on June 1, 2023 that they again are saying that they have another (third) exterminator starting on Monday in June 2023 as that is what the email below from Shelley says but there are no dates...

From: Rhona S. Kauffman
To: Stephen Steiner
Subject: RE: The Palms - Letter Regarding Rat Problem

AUGUST 20, 2023 / 6:56 PM

What date did you receive the below email? Again no dates. Please advise.

From: Rhona S. Kauffman
To: Stephen Steiner
Subject: RE: The Palms - Letter Regarding Rat Problem

AUGUST 20, 2023 / 7:02 PM

Since June 1, 2023 when you were told that there is yet a third exterminator company, has anyone reached out?

From: Rhona S. Kauffman
To: Stephen Steiner
Subject: Demand

AUGUST 21, 2023 / 1:38 PM

Please review the letter I sent last night to you so you can comment and I can serve. Thank you.

From: Stephen Steiner
To: Rhona S. Kauffman
Subject: Re: Demand

AUGUST 21, 2023 / 1:44 PM

Will do, on my way back from San Diego.

From: Rhona S. Kauffman
To: Stephen Steiner
Subject: See Attached

AUGUST 21, 2023 / 2:53 AM

Draft demand and chronology for your review and comment. Once you comment on the letter, I can serve the letter. The chronology is for only our eyes.

A SPECIAL PLACE

CHRONOLOGY

I personally created the chronology of events and organized all email correspondence for Rhona Kauffman. This was not done as a matter of convenience—but out of necessity. From the outset, each phone call with her was marked by condescension, impatience, and repeated interruptions. Rather than demonstrating empathy for the physical and emotional distress I was under, she consistently spoke to me in a rude, dismissive, and demeaning tone that only heightened my anxiety. Instead of helping me clarify the timeline, she chose to confuse and destabilize me further—often to the point where I would mentally shut down during our calls.

To avoid additional emotional strain and to reduce her hostility, I told her I would organize the timeline myself and send her a comprehensive chronology. In hindsight, this was a tactic she used to offload her responsibilities onto me while maintaining the illusion of engagement. Her behavior was not only unprofessional—it felt manipulative and intentionally degrading. I strongly believe she weaponized my vulnerable state and used it to present me as "unstable" or "difficult" in conversations with her former employer, Donna Rickman, and Shelley Westall.

Following that point, Rhona adopted an increasingly superior tone in all future conversations, speaking down to me with calculated passive-aggression. It became clear that her motives were not aligned with my best interests, but rather with shielding those responsible and keeping me disoriented and powerless. Her actions served not to advocate for me, but to break me down further when I was already unwell and desperately in need of genuine representation.

Stephen Steiner Chronology		
DATE OF EMAIL	**TO/FROM**	**CONTENT**
7/2021		Gaffney Group terminated and Seabreeze hired so never addressed- and Donna told him probably a bird or cat, then SS left for Dallas for 6 months to June 2022
7/14/22	SS to Donna Rickman at Seabreeze mgmt	unit 808 hears rodents ceiling entire community/ near a/c could eat wiring/damage: increasingly worse opening in roof from work one year ago and contacted HOA after roof work
7/14	DR to SS	issue WO pest control
7/18	SS to DR	still waiting for vender- will need access to crawl space DROPPING fell out of light fixture when changing bulb
7/18	gary bug guy to shonna obeso at seabreeze	scheduled this afternoon (Preferred Pest Control) with SS
7/20	SS to DR	pest guy came and checked roof openings. Said maybe neighbors; getting worse; up all night from noise; contact pest control again
	DR to SS	will check and find out next step
	SS to DR	pest guy said if a unit vacant the toilet water evaporates and rats climb up
9/6	SS to DR	rat problem still here running day night all over ceiling; rat droppings in crawl space need to be checked and removed; opening somewhere
9/11	SS to DR	issue horrendous all hours; video hear rats running in crawl space; sees rat dropping in light fixtures; need someone now to make hole in crawl space to remove rats clean up; scared to open all cabinets kitchens etc Unhealthy; concern for air quality as well
9/12	SS to DR	now in AC unit crawling in tubes and one fell on unit in hallway, need sanitation of AC: SEND SOMONE OR SS WILL FIND SOMEONE AND SEND BILL TO HOA Sleeping on couch going insane
9/30	DR to SS and Giuseppe (neighbor)	give dates next week to meet with exterminator and DR
	G to DR	Friday afternoon or Saturday
	SS to DR and G	anytime available
	DR to SS	Giuseppe available Fridays exterminator
10/5	SS to DR	have roof opened up to let rats out, they are back and going insane, resolve now, ceiling needs to be replaced
10/6	DR to SS and G	Friday appt. confirmed,
10/7	same	
10/13	SS to DR	pleasure meeting you; checking on exterminator to open ceiling PDF ATTACHED ??
10/14	DR to SS	coordinating estimate for cut and service door with HANDYMAN. According to matrix, homeowner responsible for paying for cut and service door. HOA pays for inspection and traps. SS has to agree with DR. VEZZOLI on estimate.
	SS to DR and G	why he wanted opening on roof. Did not want responsibility to pay since rats coming from roof.
	DR to SS and G	Corey said service door needs to be ordered and cost 250.00. Then sent estimate SUBJECT TO CHANGE
	SS to DR and G	Why not roof? Came from outside, estimate only and already paying 430 for HOA dues MORE ATTACHMENTS
10/16	SS to DR and G	URGENT rats made HOLE in pipe and water falling down and being absorbed in padding; water stain on wall; UNIT humid and smells rancid; water used to clean upholstery was yellow; rat urine seeping down walls water dripping on ceiling and unit smells; furniture damaged; two years and came from roof outside HANTVIRUS relocation
10/19	SS to DR and G	handyman did not show up yesterday
	DR to SS and G	Plumber here yesterday, waiting on Board approval
10/23	DR to SS and G	Directed by board to obtain second opinion with another pest control provider;
	G to DR and SS	SS has key and can enter
	SS to DR and G	SECOND OPINION?? --- Living with rats for past 1 ½ years droppings in light fixtures, hear every night; going crazy;
11/8	SS to DR	board quote approved so schedule opening
	DR to SS	waiting for access door
11/14	DR to SS	available for installation of access door **different email from DD states temporary cut made on Monday 11/14 and then closed up due to problems with location (see below in email from SS)
11/15	SS to DR and G	NEW FAMILY OF RATS MOVED IN LOUD AND RUNNING AROUND ENTIRE CEILING attached video
	G to DR and SS	video of SS attic conditions/noise above kitchen. My unit same condition rat droppings urine unhealthy EXTERMINATOR INCOMPETENT THIS SHOULD BE PRIORITY HEATLH ISSUE. SS and I very patient (some board mem don't live here) or we handle send HOA bill
11/16	DR to SS and G	DR, Jordan from Preferred Pest Ctl met to install access door in primary bedroom so Jordan could set rat traps. Also wkr from Vantage Construction to install access door. Wkr reviewed cut made and closed Monday 11/14 needs frame. DR offered to go to home depot SS said didnt want access door in bedroom closet and that SS will install himself a plastic door in his bedroom by Friday 11/18. Jordan said cut would work if not obstructed by air ducts or pipes. Doors is temp and wall will be returned once rat problem resolved.
11/17	DR to SS	confirm SS will install access door. HOA not doing install. HOA will provide abatement service
11/18	SS to DR and G	confused by email sounds like SS delaying but not. SS wrote lengthy email ***ON 11/14/22** Corey Handyman arrived 10 am didnt complete until 4:30pm. *original hole not planned well, Corey made hole in closet at exterminator direction but pipes directly above so bad hole location. Should have used infrared gun. *SS and Corey contacted DR and sent pictures with new location for approval by Jordan. *Also video of rat droppings *project cancelled and hole patched *Trap doors ordered not suited for this and instead for electrical boxes on a vertical wall- doors heavy and need to be attached to wooden frame. With correct trap door and right location, a one hour job instead of 6 hrs. ***ON 11/16/22** Jordon his boss and you came over to find new place for installation. Jordan decided to reopen the hole and add wooden frame to attach trap door. Wkr Vantage construction was not told instructions and DR left, he was going to just screw door on to drywall with no opening. No one gave him directions to reopen and build a frame first. **That is why SS volunteered to do installation**. He was incompetent and no directions *then SS INCORPORATED 7/22 EMAIL *been over 5 months rodent invasion *states damages sustained - stress, disgust, sleepless nights, heath hazard inhalation particles from urine droppings
11/28	DR to G *not attached	Bd passed comprehensive plan for eradicating rats. Attached plan but only to G not to SS. Plan to place trap door with inhouse company installation and temporay to erradicate rats BOARD REJECTS GOING THROUGH ROOF WARRANTY AND WATER LEAKS EXPENSE
	DR to SS	Bd passed comprehensive plan for eradicating rats. Attached plan but only to G not to SS. Plan to place trap door with inhouse company installation and temporay to erradicate rats then restored to original condition. DR will have point person for project contact SS. BOARD REJECTS GOING THROUGH ROOF WARRANTY AND WATER LEAKS EXPENSE
	G to DR	Happy board approved rat exclusion plan
	SS to DR	SS will allow them to place trap door if professionals and requests number of person who collects traps. If hears one go off wants them there asap. Every evening rats come out of pipes at back patio area and run down ceiling in closet When done who will clean up crawl space?
	SS to G	SS approved them to enter his unit and offer G to get key to enter G unit
11/30	DR to SS	availability for tomorrow 2:30 pm trap door installation utility closet checked and closed Shane Western Extermin 4 pm installation?
	SS to DR	4 good
12/7	SS to DR	She has bulbs
1/23/23	SS to DR	Rat situation worse still getting in crawl space, making noise and damage, tired of living this way dangerous chew wire cause fire hazardous
2/7	SS to DR	rat problem incredibly bad; activity worse than before; rats attacking rats and baby rats; chasing fighting; four hours; entire unit reeks of rat urine; HOA pay rental, utility, moving remove ceiling and all insulation, santize crawspace, air ducts, replace carpet, repaint unit, horrible headaches; decrease in property value will not pay dues until repaired before summer heat
2/8	DR to SS and Shelley Westall and Gary Fritzen	Requested report from Nick at Western Exterm including documentation servicing SS unit: Nick will call SS to pick up footage from camera in crawl space to review and develop plan SS may be displaced but should not pay for accommodations **Western reviewed footage of crawl space and new action plan for extermination that may displace you
2/9	SS to DR	big concern clean up
2/28	HOA to SS	board considered next steps after neighbor advised at 2/25 bod meeting that ongoing rodent problems and email and video. On 2/27 DR emailed Western exter oper mgr Chad McChesney to inspect and treat attic and SS unit for ongoing conditions preventing eradication. Chad will personally inspect unit and review camera placement. **Made several attempts to reach SS.** Board taken extroditary steps to treat and prevent rodent intrusion Hired two exterminators cut access points in ceiling, sealed ingress areas, blocked outdoor access points by removing foilage and mature trees. Western reports no current indications of rats in living space of his unit. SS only resident reporting problem so cooperation mandatory. Thursday March 2, 2023 Western inspection. If no response then board cannot proceed and consider the issue resolved.
3/1	SS to DR and Shelly Westall	allow exterminator into property. Already done many times over last yr. Nick used to inspect from Western. SS No information about what was recorded by Nick. Unbelievable that SS camera records rodents but exterminator does not. Erradication never happened. Primary conecer should be preventing rats from entering. Not erradicating. Nick Chad and others repeadedly checked utility closet in both units and crawlspace but no result. And gave Chad tour to inspect all entry ways. NO IMMEDIATE AND EXTRAORDINARY STEPS. what are they???? Western has not check SS unit in over one month. **Bd considering resolved if SS does not respond in two days!????**
3/2	DR to SS	Western appt 3/3/23
3/13	DR to SS SS to DR DR to SS	Improvement? Trapped rats running around dying off When is clean up? After 100 percent eradicated
3/24 3/25	DR to SS SS to DR	Status? NEW ONES ENTERED
4/4 4/5	DR to SS SS to DR	Western place access door in master bedroom closet APPROVE
4/21	DR to SS SS to DR	improving is access installed? SLIGHTLY BETTER BUT STILL THERE
5/31	SS	New GM Donna Left
6/1	Shelly Westall to SS	no current CCRs since 80s. She hasnt seen rat exclusion plan
8/9	SS	Received call from Seabreeze under impression over
8/14	SS	rats still present RAT INFESTATION CRAWLSPACE LITTERED WITH RAT DROPPINGS AND URINE. SMELL, URINE FECES AND RODENTS THREE SEPARATE ENTRY POINTS INTO CEILING AND NONE SEALED UP, VIDEO FOOTAGE
	*prevelent thorugh entire ceiling with focus in kitchen nests everywhere	*entire removal of all urine.. Fecus, rodents and their nestsand replacement of entire ceiling *insulation *sanitization *a/c system replaced- rats fell into closet where it is located *mental breakdown medication *urine and fecus uncomprehensible *never hired the right exterminator expert *numerous exterminators from different companies *toxic environment *heat smell incomprehensible

Adding to the frustration, whenever I sent her images or video evidence, she often claimed she couldn't view the attachments or play the files. During one meeting in the shared conference room, I asked whether she had reviewed the materials. She became visibly flustered, struggling to operate her email system and unable to locate my messages. Ironically, I had created a dedicated email account specifically for this case to ensure all correspondence would be easy to access. I ended up showing her how to search for my emails — a basic task for someone in her position. For an attorney who claimed to have worked on the O.J. Simpson case, her performance was, at best, a poor imitation of competence.

From: Stephen Steiner
To: Rhona S. Kauffman
Subject: Re: Demand

AUGUST 21, 2023 / 4:22 PM

It's all perfect. There is one typo of my name.

From: Rhona S. Kauffman
To: Stephen Steiner
Subject: RE: Demand

AUGUST 21, 2023 / 5:36 PM

Ok sounds good just let me know when you have reviewed and if you approve or it needs any factual changes.

From: Stephen Steiner
To: Rhona S. Kauffman
Subject: Re: See Attached

AUGUST 21, 2023 / 5:39 PM

Looks great! Three changes. Three typos that I saw.

The second to last paragraph starts "Then in February…" My name is spelled Mr. Steinman twice. And at the very end, the cc says Stephan Steiner. Other than that it is perfect.

Please send it to the HOA and Seabreeze.

Of course, I returned from San Diego and my AC unit was not working. The storm caused it to short out. The AC repair man believes it could be an exposed wire. I bet it was something the rats chewed up. He thought it was something internal that went bad but when he replaced the transformer it shorted again and most likely is something on the roof which he is currently checking out. It burned out my Ecobee.

From: Rhona S. Kauffman
To: Stephen Steiner
Subject: Re: See Attached

AUGUST 21, 2023 / 6:33 PM

So sorry about the three spelling errors. That's why I send to my clients and then I do a final spellcheck review. Also, I think I forwarded you that chronology that took me several hours to put together but it's very helpful moving forward. I will serve the letter I have made the corrections and I will forward you the final.

From: Rhona S. Kauffman
To: Stephen Steiner
Subject: FOR YOUR FILE

AUGUST 21, 2023 / 7:31 PM

YES I WILL LET YOU KNOW WHEN WE RECEIVE A RESPONSE.

It took from June 4th until August 21st for Rhona to issue a demand letter to the HOA's attorneys—an extensive and unexplained delay. Considering the urgency and severity of the situation, such prolonged inaction raises serious concerns and gives the appearance of intentional stalling. And misspelling my name twice? I suspect she wrote this dictating or purposely did to annoy and anger me. Rude.

From: Stephen Steiner
To: Rhona S. Kauffman
Subject: Re: FOR YOUR FILE

AUGUST 21, 2023 / 7:44 PM

The rats are officially back. As soon as I sent the last email one of them either fell off a stud or was running through the crawlspace.

SERVING SAN DIEGO:

PROSPECT BUSINESS CENTER
888 PROSPECT ST.
SUITE 200
LA JOLLA, CA 92037

RHONA S. KAUFFMAN
LAW OFFICES OF RHONA S. KAUFFMAN

SERVING PALM DESERT:

PARC EXECUTIVE SUITES
BUILDING A
77564 COUNTRY CLUB DR.
SUITE 115
PALM DESERT, CA 92211

TELEPHONE: (760) 772-8225
FACSIMILE: (760) 406-5095
EMAIL: RKAUFFMAN@RHONAKAUFFMANLAW.COM

August 21, 2023

Served Via Certified U. S. Mail
THE PALMS HOMEOWNERS ASSOCIATION
C/O Wayne S. Guralnick, Esq.
Guralnick & Gilliland, LLP
40-004 Cook Street, Suite 3
Palm Desert, CA 92211

Subject:	**Member Stephen Steiner - 3155 E. Ramon Road, Unit 808 Palm Springs ("Unit")**
Re:	**Rodent Infestation**

Dear Mr. Guralnick:

Please be advised that Mr. Stephen Steiner, a member of THE PALMS HOMEOWNERS ASSOCIATION ("HOA"), has retained my law office to represent his legal interests in connection with the HOA's failure to properly maintain, repair, replace, and sanitize a portion of the Common Area, namely the crawl space, the insulation, and ceiling in Mr. Steiner's Unit. Over the course of two years, and specifically this past year, Mr. Steiner has been subjected to a serious rat infestation leading to an extremely toxic environment affecting my Client's physical and emotional health. Additionally, this rat infestation has caused and continues to cause extensive property damage within the Unit. Moreover, Mr. Steiner, his family members, guests and other members of the HOA continue to be subjected to this ongoing and horrendous health hazard.

The purpose of this correspondence is to demand that the HOA immediately take action to permanently eradicate all rodents, and then replace the entire ceiling and flooring in the Unit including the insulation etc, and the Air Condition Unit, and finally sanitize the entire Unit. You may direct all further communications to the undersigned in this regard. Time is of the Essence.

At all relevant times, the HOA confirmed and assumed the duty to maintain the crawlspace Common Area above Mr. Steiner's Unit in accordance with the provisions set forth in the Declaration of Establishment of Covenants, Conditions and Restrictions for The Palms recorded on August 13, 1980. This infestation began shortly after the HOA retained a roof vendor to open up and repair the roof above Mr. Steiner's Unit in July 2021.

As a result of the HOA's breach of the Governing Documents, the Directors' Breach of their fiduciary duties in maintaining the Common Area, as well as serious negligence in diligently eradicating the rodents (after assuming the duty to protect Mr. Steiner from this infestation), my Client has been subjected to many sleepless nights and sustained voluminous property damage. Mr. Steiner lays awake many nights listening to numerous rat families squeaking and scurrying around in the ceiling, worrying about his toxic environment and whether a rat will fall through the ceiling or fall into the closet (*yes this happened*) or rat droppings falling from the light fixtures (*and this*). Literally, the walls and some carpet areas are saturated with rat urine. This horrendous situation over the course of this past two years has traumatized Mr. Steiner who was forced to seek medical attention for his fragile mental state and emotional distress.

Page 1 of 4

RHONA S. KAUFFMAN
Law offices of Rhona S. Kauffman

Our investigation has confirmed the following:

Mr. Steiner placed the HOA on notice of this rodent infestation in the crawl space of his Unit back in 2021 after the HOA completed roof repairs. Donna Rickman, the Property Manager at Seabreeze Management, brushed off Mr. Steiner telling him it was probably a cat or bird on the roof. Then in July 2022, the infestation of rodents became increasingly obvious and toxic. On July 14, 2022, Mr. Steiner again informed Ms. Rickman about the entire community of rodents running around his ceiling. He also expressed concern in his email about potential damage to the wiring in his Unit from the rats. A work order was issued for Preferred Pest Control.

On July 20, 2022, the Pest Control came to investigate by checking the roof for openings. Mr. Steiner was not privy to the report of the investigation. Nothing happened and the HOA did not follow-up.

On September 6, 2022, and again on September 11 & 12, 2022, Mr. Steiner emailed Ms. Rickman about the rodents running all day and night all over the ceiling and rat droppings in the crawl space. He also forwarded audios of rats running in the crawl space and videos of rat droppings in the light fixtures. Mr. Steiner requested the HOA to immediately retain an expert to make an opening in the crawl space in his ceiling to remove the rats and sanitize the Unit. He had major concerns about the air quality as well as fears about finding rats in his cabinets. Additionally, he notified Ms. Rickman about a rat that fell on the Air Conditioner in the hallway.

On September 30, 2022, Ms. Rickman finally responded to Mr. Steiner and his neighbor, Giuseppe who was also experiencing the same rodent infestation, telling them in an email that another exterminator would once again meet to investigate the following week.

On October 5, 2022, Mr. Steiner stressed to Ms. Rickman that the ceiling needed to be replaced and the roof had to be opened up so the rats could exit permanently. Of course the HOA is responsible for maintenance and repairs to the roof and this whole rat infestation began with the HOA roof repairs back in July 2021. However, the HOA refused to do any roof investigation at all and refused to hire a roof contractor to investigate and repair the rodent roof access. It was very apparent that the rats were and are still entering from the roof yet the HOA refused and continues to refuse to address the source of this rat infestation on the roof. Instead, an estimate was prepared by the Handyman for the HOA, to cut into the ceiling of the Unit and place a service door in the ceiling to access the crawl space. Not only did the HOA say that my Client was required to pay for the cut and service door but they were using an unlicensed Handyman to cut into my Client's ceiling.

On October 14, 2022, three months after my Client first notified the HOA of this disastrous situation, Ms. Rickman told Mr. Steiner and Giuseppe that the Handyman said it takes time to order a service door for the ceiling. Again my Client inquired about a roof investigation but was ignored.

On October 16, 2022, again Mr. Steiner emailed Ms. Rickman and cc'd Giuseppe "URGENT" the rats punctured the pipes and water was falling down staining the walls and being absorbed in the carpet padding. To Mr. Steiner's horror and dismay, the water was yellow, and the entire Unit smelled rancid from the rat urine seeping down the walls onto the furniture and carpet. No response to this Urgent email.

Then on October 19, 2022, the Handyman failed to show up. When Mr. Steiner notified Ms. Rickman, she responded that she is waiting on the HOA approval and that she was directed to obtain a second opinion. Of course, Mr. Steiner was horrified as he had been living with these rodents for the past 1 1/2 years and in fear for his health, safety and well-being.

RHONA S. KAUFFMAN
Law offices of Rhona S. Kauffman

Finally on or about November 8, 2022, now four months after Mr. Steiner notified Ms. Rickman again of the severity of the ongoing infestation, a date for installation of the access door was scheduled.

On November 14, 2022, since the HOA refused to investigate the roof access, my Client allowed Corey, the Handyman to make a cut in the ceiling to access the crawl space. Unfortunately, he was not a licensed contractor and did not verify that the location of the cut in the Unit ceiling was a good location to install traps etc. After the cut was made, it was determined that there were problems with the location due to obstructions of air ducts and pipes. An infrared gun would have made that determination in advance of cutting into my Client's ceiling at random. Photos of rats and droppings were sent however to the HOA from that access cut. Also noted is that Corey spent 6 hours with my Client that day on a job that should have only taken one hour with a licensed contractor.

Over the next few weeks, several emails were exchanged between my Client and Ms. Rickman. Specifically, Mr. Steiner continuously complained about the elevated noise, the scurrying of the numerous rats in the ceiling crawl space every night and the toxic conditions of his Unit. He attached videos depicting the crawl space conditions above the kitchen of rats, rat urine and rat droppings. Giuseppe also chimed in to Ms. Rickman repeating all of my Client's complaints and concerns and referencing the incompetent exterminators.

Finally on November 16, 2022, Preferred Pest Control showed up with Ms. Rickman at Mr. Steiner's residence to install an access door in the primary bedroom so traps could be set. Unfortunately more incompetence as it was determined that the cut needed a frame in order to install the access door. Of course no one had a frame in hand. And the person from Vantage Construction was not given the proper instructions and attempted to screw the access door on to the drywall without a frame which of course was not possible. Incompetent. Also my Client did not want an access door to the rats in his bedroom, who would??? And most important, this was four months later, from July 2022, that my Client had been enduring this terrible nightmare. He suffered and continues to suffer from stress, depression and sleepless nights not to mention the significant health hazards from inhalation of the particles from the urine and rat droppings.

Although the HOA allegedly passed a "comprehensive plan for eradicating the rats" on November 28, 2022, (*email from Ms. Rickman to Giuseppe attaching this "plan"*) no plan was attached to any email or implemented. And in that same email, Ms. Rickman confirmed that the HOA again rejected investigating and going through the roof to eradicate the rat infestation.

Then in February, Western Exterminators came to the Unit and reviewed the camera from the crawl space. An operating manager, Chad McChesney inspected the Unit but of course the rodents live on in my Client's ceiling. Western placed an access door in the master bedroom closet but to date, no plan has been implemented to eradicate the rodents and to date, Mr. Steiner suffers emotionally, mentally and physically as a result of being subjected to this toxic environment. The property damage is significant and Mr. Steiner has been prevented from selling his Unit. This is directly related to the HOA's negligence and Breach of Fiduciary Duty in failing to hire a licensed roof contractor, in hiring incompetent workers and unlicenced workers and incompetent pest control companies.

While a board is granted Judicial Deference in determining how the common areas are to be maintained, an HOA may be held liable for its failure to investigate maintenance problems and to take reasonable action. A homeowners' association has a fiduciary relationship with its members.[I]n recognition of the increasingly important role played by private homeowners' associations...the courts have recognized that such associations owe a fiduciary duty to their members. (Cohen v. Kite Hill Community Assn. (1983) 142 Cal.App.3d. 642, 650-651.)

Page 3 of 4

THE LONG AWAITED DEMAND LETTER

RHONA S. KAUFFMAN
Law offices of Rhona S. Kauffman

Board members also have a duty to act with the utmost good faith and reasonable care for the benefit of the association and its members. Directors of nonprofit corporations such as this HOA are fiduciaries who are required to exercise their powers in accordance with the duties imposed by the Corporation Code and the Davis-Stirling Common Interest Development Act. This fiduciary relationship is governed by the statutory standard that requires directors to exercise due care and undivided loyalty for the interests of the corporation. (Frances T. v. Village Green Owners Assn. (1986) 42 Cal.3d 490, 513.)

Directors must also be diligent and careful in performing the duties they have undertaken. (Burt v. Irvine Company (1965) 237 Cal.App.2d 828). Directors must specifically enforce the governing documents. Unfortunately the HOA has failed in its duties and obligations in this regard. Here, there was no reasonable action taken over the course of two years to retain roof experts eradicate the rodents and clean up and sanitize the Unit.

This correspondence shall serve as a demand for the HOA to immediately take action to permanently eradicate all rodents, hire roofing experts, and then replace the entire ceiling and flooring in the Unit including the insulation etc, and the Air Condition Unit, and finally sanitize the entire Unit. My Client has sustained significant damages and Loss of Use of his Unit.

Otherwise, this shall serve as a demand to Mediate this dispute in accordance with the Davis-Stirling Common Interest Development Act as to why the HOA is failing to maintain the common area and properly investigate as required by the governing documents.

Nothing in this correspondence constitutes any waiver of my Client's rights in law or in equity, all of which are expressly reserved. We look forward to amicably resolving this matter.

Very truly yours,
RHONA S. KAUFFMAN
Rhona S. Kauffman, Esq.

cc: Stephen Steiner

Page 4 of 4

A SPECIAL PLACE

From: Stephen Steiner
To: Rhona S. Kauffman
Subject: Action Needed

For the past 2 years living here I have had numerous rashes and breakouts. I assumed it was the stress. My back, elbows, hands, chest, have gotten rashes throughout the 2 years. I was in San Diego for 4 days. My back is in constant breakout. Mostly water blisters. My hand and elbows have had strange rashes that I finally found out was ringworm. I shouldn't be getting ringworm…. I don't have any pets, except for the rats!!

The four days I was in San Diego my back almost cleared up. Got back yesterday and this morning it is covered in itchy blisters. Even the top of my head has them. I know these are not shingles because I am on Valtrex. The rat urine and feces is the cause.

I am attaching pictures of what inhaling rat urine and poop do to a human.

They need to move me into an Airbnb fast. I am so tired of these skin problems. I am going to see my doctor to make sure it has not triggered some other illness. If they say they won't please file a lawsuit for millions. I can't take anymore. They have ruined my life.

Please let them know they will be packing up all my belongings and putting into storage and moving me somewhere that will not make me sick.

I don't want to be in this condo anymore. It is toxic. I am including a picture of what i looked like when I moved back in. Donna destroyed my home, life, and body. I wish I could ask her if she is proud of how she treated another human. The Board and Seabreeze should be forced to live in my condo so they can experience what I am going through.

Before the rodent infestation began, I had launched a new business. It was gaining momentum until my health began to deteriorate due to the toxic conditions in my condo. The sleepless nights, extreme stress, and the ongoing disregard for my well-being by Shelley Westall, Donna Rickman, the Board of Directors, and Seabreeze Management severely impacted my ability to work and function.

Despite this, I pushed forward with preparations for the San Diego tattoo convention, where I had secured a booth to promote my brand. It was an incredibly challenging time—my shingles outbreaks, combined with mounting psychological stress, made it difficult to stay focused. But I managed to pull through.

While I was in San Diego, I began to feel physical relief. My symptoms started to clear, and the skin conditions I had been struggling with began to heal. The connection was undeniable: being away from the contaminated condo had a direct and positive effect on my health.

However, the moment I returned, I was overwhelmed by the stench of decaying rodents. The temperature inside the unit was over 100°, while outside it had reached 120° due to a brutal summer heat wave. Hurricane Hilary had just passed through Palm Springs, leaving the air thick with humidity. I was immediately puzzled as to why the air conditioning hadn't been running. I had installed an Ecobee thermostat over a year prior and had programmed it to maintain a consistent indoor temperature of 75° during the summer.

When I checked the device, I found that it was completely nonfunctional. Upon removing it from the wall, I discovered that the internal components had melted, as if the unit had shorted out. At the time, I assumed the storm may have caused the failure. I spoke with neighboring homeowners to confirm whether there had been power outages or lightning strikes—but none had experienced any electrical issues during or after the storm.

This raised serious questions. The damage could have been caused by a rodent chewing through wiring, a rat falling into the HVAC system and causing a short, someone tampering with the system from the roof, or a direct lightning strike to my unit. The true cause remains unknown, but the timing and circumstances were deeply suspicious.

From: Stephen Steiner
To: Rhona S. Kauffman
Subject: Update

Any response from the lawyers? I do not want to live in this condo anymore. Been sick and the stress from living in it is making me even worse. I don't want to play a waiting game with them. I am miserable and want to get out of this place.

A SPECIAL PLACE

I suspect it'll take a couple weeks till we hear something, but I will let you know when the letter was received because it was sent certified.

A couple of weeks? I was living in a rat-infested, toxic environment—something every one of them knew—and I was told it would take a couple of weeks just to get a response. Meanwhile, my health was deteriorating, and I was barely functioning. This wasn't a scheduling issue; it was a calculated tactic. Yet another deliberate delay, designed to wear me down while they continued to do nothing.

Thank you.

Been doing some research to see what is happening to me. When I was in San Diego my symptoms were clearing up and the day after I got back they started up again. It causes me massive depression and has continued to ruin my life.

I didn't realize but I have what looks like some kind of fungus on my tattooed hand. Sending pics to Dr too. I started getting strange water/blood blisters that would pop as soon as I scratched them. They are very itchy. I also noticed that for some weird reason, my thumbnail started getting a fungus that is killing it off. It has already destroyed 6 of my toenails. And tonight a new blister on the back of my ear.

I had none of this when I moved back in two years ago. It has been getting worse every day. Please let them know what torture they are putting me through and I now want to sue them for physical damage. I am a disgusting infection. I want them to pay for what they are still doing to me. They need to move me out immediately. They are killing me.

Please send them the pictures and make sure Donna and Shelley see them too. They have destroyed my life.

Any damage to tattoos they will cover cost to fix and the additional suffering I had to go through and the pain I will go through to have repaired.

I apologize having to show you these pics. I am gross.

From: Stephen Steiner
To: Rhona S. Kauffman
Subject: Pics didn't attach. Big surprise...Android

AUGUST 26, 2023 / 11:11 PM

Pics didn't attach. Big surprise...Android. Here they are.

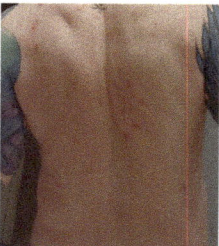

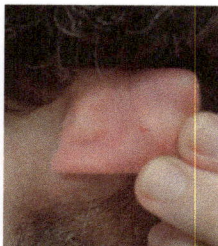

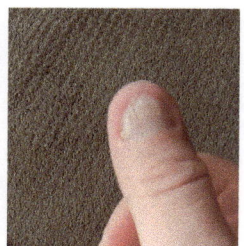

A SPECIAL PLACE

From: Rhona S. Kauffman
To: Stephen Steiner
Subject: RE: Pics didn't attach. Big surpirse...Android

AUGUST 28, 2023 / 3:28 PM

WHAT IS ON YOUR BACK? DID YOU GO TO DOCTOR? PLEASE GO AND FORWARD DOCTOR'S NOTES

From: Rhona S. Kauffman
To: Stephen Steiner
Subject: RE: Pics didn't attach. Big surprise...Android

AUGUST 28, 2023 / 3:29 PM

I am not sure what you are showing me? please advise

It became painfully clear that she either wasn't reading my emails at all or was merely glancing over them as if they were unimportant. I had provided detailed explanations and included photographs documenting the severity of my condition—shingles across my back and a spreading fungal infection—yet there was no meaningful acknowledgment. The lack of response made it obvious that what I was going through wasn't being taken seriously.

From: Rhona S. Kauffman
To: Stephen Steiner
Subject: RE: Pictures of what I go through every day

AUGUST 28, 2023 / 3:30 PM

Ok. I read the below. Please send doctor's notes after your appointment.

From: Stephen Steiner
To: Rhona S. Kauffman
Subject: Re: Pictures of what I go through every day

AUGUST 29, 2023 / 4:47 PM

Will do.

From: Stephen Steiner
To: Rhona S. Kauffman
Subject: Re: Pictures of what I go through every day

AUGUST 30, 2023 / 12:30 PM

I am waiting in a urgent care because of Donna. Palm Springs is nothing but a continuous nightmare for me. Nothing goes my way.

Everything has to be difficult and always ten times more difficult for me. Because of complete incompetence of the HOA and Seabreeze I have to endure the physical and mental damage they have purposely put me through.

It's so wonderful that Donna was transfered to another property while I suffer with the virus from rats running through my body. I hope she enjoys living in her beautiful home while I sit in my rat infested home inhaling feces and urine.

I forgot to include the entire HOA Board. I can only hope they and Donna get to experience living with rats above their heads for two years. Spending those warm summer days and nights smelling the rancid oder seeping from their ceilings.

I would love to be the exterminator coming to their homes and doing nothing, dragging the infestation month to month to month till they go insane. Insure they would love to experience how all their friends and neighbors avoid being seen with them. Isolating their lives to sitting in their homes to wait for the rats to find a way in.

And when they beg me to do something I will email a "?"

A SPECIAL PLACE

It took me three different Immediate Care facilities to finally get in. It is like everyone in Palm Springs has no clue about what their job is and randomly give out incorrect information.

So the diagnosis I received:

Ringworm - Not sure how I would get ringworm since I am not in contact with anyone and have OCD so every inch of my home is spotless...oh wait...rats.

Urticaria - Hives — also called urticaria (ur-tih-KAR-e-uh) — is a skin reaction that causes itchy welts. Chronic hives are welts that last for more than six weeks and return often over months or years. Often, the cause of chronic hives isn't clear - but in this case, rats.

Quote "While we cannot make a direct correlation between the rats and your rash, the stress of the situation can certainly cause a rash like this."

I am also attaching a copy of the visit report. Any response from their attorneys?

DESERT OASIS HEALTHCARE

DOHC IC PS
275 N El Cielo Road Suite D402
Palm Springs, CA 92262-6972
Phone: (760)969-5888 Fax: (760)969-7245

PATIENT PLAN FOR 8/29/2023

Patient:	Stephen Steiner
Date of Birth:	
Date of Visit:	08/29/2023 05:30 PM
Visit Type:	Immediate Care Visit
Rendering provider:	Andrew Miller
Location:	DOHC IC PS
Immediate Care/Call us here:	**(760)969-5888**
24/7 Nurse Helpline:	**(760)969-6555**

Have an urgent medical issue? Please come visit us at one of our four Immediate Care locations below. We are open weekends and holidays!

- Immediate Care Palm Springs, Indio, Immediate Care Palm Desert, and Yucca Valley
  - Monday - Friday: 8am - 8pm
  - Weekends and Holidays: 9am - 7pm

Thank you for choosing us for your healthcare needs. The following is a summary of the outcome of today's visit. If your symptoms do not improve, please come and visit us. Call us for any questions or concerns!

MEDICATIONS *Sent Today.* Please call us if you are unable to pick up below medication -
On Aug 29 2023 5:56PM AndrewM sent Medrol (Pak) 4 mg tablets in a dose pack via Electronic to CVS PHARMACY-PALM SPRINGS - 425 S Sunrise Way, Palm Springs
On Aug 29 2023 6:00PM AndrewM sent Diflucan 150 mg tablet via Electronic to CVS PHARMACY-PALM SPRINGS - 425 S Sunrise Way, Palm Springs

REASON(S) FOR VISIT
Rash to body.

Assessment Plan

1.	Assessment	Ringworm (B35.9), Acute.
2.	Assessment	Urticaria (L50.9), Acute.
	Patient Plan	Start the Medrol pack tomorrow as you got a full day's dose of steroids in the shot today. Take the Diflucan once a week for 10 weeks. You should try to get in to see a dermatologist especially if this persists. While we cannot make a direct correlation between the rats and your rash, the stress of the situation can certainly cause a rash like this.
	Plan Orders	The patient had the following medication order(s) completed today: Solumedrol/125 mg IM. Obtained on 08/29/2023, Dose 125 mg via IM on left buttock.

Steiner, Stephen   000000757957 10/25/1968 08/29/2023 05:30 PM Page: 1/3

As a direct result of the ongoing negligence by the HOA and Seabreeze Management, I was forced to endure constant physical suffering. I experienced repeated outbreaks of shingles and a fungal infection that spread across my body, eventually affecting my fingernails. These were not isolated incidents—these conditions persisted throughout the entire ordeal. The shingles progressively worsened, spreading toward my ears and face. Had it reached my eyes, it could have resulted in permanent blindness.

Despite the seriousness of my condition, there was no meaningful concern expressed by anyone involved—including Rhona. My declining health was treated with indifference, as though it were a minor inconvenience rather than the life-altering consequence of their inaction.

Mo	Tu	We	Th	Fr	Sa	Su
				1	2	3
4	5	6	7	8	9	10
11	12	13	14	15	16	17
18	19	20	21	22	23	24
25	26	27	28	29	30	

SEPTEMBER

444 DAYS
UNRESOLVED

From: Rhona S. Kauffman
To: Stephen Steiner
Subject: Fwd: Our client: The Palms HOA; Your client: Steiner

SEPTEMBER 1, 2023 / 8:51 AM

The HOA attorneys responded and are investigating. I will let you know when I hear back from them. Thank you.

> From: Marilyn Ramos
> To: Rhona S. Kauffman
> Cc: Wayne Guralnick
> Subject: Our client: The Palms HOA; Your client: Steiner
>
> *SEPTEMBER 1, 2023 / 6:49 AM*
>
> We wanted to let you know that we are in receipt of your letter. We have been retained by the HOA to handle the matter and respond to you. We are in the process of obtaining all information/documentation regarding the incident and the allegations in your letter. We will respond to your letter upon completion of our due diligence anticipated to take one to two weeks.

It's astonishing how everything conveniently seemed to take "two weeks." After more than a year of documented suffering, Rhona—who was hired to advocate on my behalf—should have been leveraging her legal expertise to demand immediate action or threaten litigation to compel urgency. Instead, she fell in line with the same pattern of excuses and delays I had already been subjected to by the HOA and Seabreeze. Her inaction was not only unacceptable—it was complicit.

From: Rhona S. Kauffman
To: Marilyn Ramos
Cc: Wayne Guralnick
Subject: Re: Our client: The Palms HOA; Your client: Steiner

SEPTEMBER 8, 2023 / 1:11 PM

Good afternoon, please note my client is terrified and living in a horrible situation with the rodents running rampant. Please advise as to when you anticipate a response will be provided.

This email makes it unmistakably clear that she was not invested in my case. It took her an entire week to respond to opposing counsel—a delay that speaks volumes about her lack of urgency, commitment, and professional responsibility.

From: Stephen Steiner
To: Rhona S. Kauffman
Subject: Any Update?

SEPTEMBER 9, 2023 / 3:58 PM

Sorry to keep bothering you about my situation. I am extremely exhausted. How long does this "investigation" take? I have rats, there is video evidence, there are witnesses. They are making me suffer for a reason I cannot figure out. None of this is my fault.

Very Depressed

A SPECIAL PLACE

From: Rhona S. Kauffman
To: Stephen Steiner
Subject: FW: Our client: The Palms HOA; Your client: Steiner

Good morning, I had already emailed the attorney on Friday (see below) before I received your Saturday email. Please see below his response on Friday:

> From: Wayne Guralnick
> To: Rhona S. Kauffman
> Cc: Marilyn Ramos
> Subject: RE: Our client: The Palms HOA; Your client: Steiner
>
> *SEPTEMBER 8, 2023 / 1:21 PM*
>
> Good afternoon Rhona:
>
> We are checking with the pest control vendor but the information we have to date is that there are no rodents and there have not been any for some time. That is part of the due diligence we are pursuing to verify same and as we indicated in our prior email, we would get back to you by end of next week.
>
> Wayne Guralnick
>
> Guralnick & Gilliland, LLP
> A Full Service Community Association Law Firm Providing Practical Solutions

First, I'd like to thank you, Rhona, for waiting three days to inform me of their response—despite receiving the email the same day. That delay alone speaks volumes.

As for the content of the response itself, it was undeniable proof that this was a deliberate and cruel game. "No rodents"? That claim is either a result of willful ignorance on the part of Wayne Guralnick or a clear indication that none of the evidence was ever shared with him. I know for a fact he never contacted a single pest control vendor. Every exterminator who entered my unit was visibly disturbed that I was still living in such toxic, uninhabitable conditions. His statement wasn't just false—it was either grossly negligent or intentionally deceptive.

From: Stephen Steiner
To: Rhona S. Kauffman
Subject: FW: Our client: The Palms HOA; Your client: Steiner

Incredible.

And I have magic beans.

From: Marilyn Ramos
To: Wayne Guralnick, Rhona S. Kauffman
Subject: FW: Our client: The Palms HOA; Your client: Steiner

Rhona,

Good Evening. Please see attached response and documentation.

From: Rhona S. Kauffman
To: Stephen Steiner
Subject: FW: Our client: The Palms HOA; Your client: Steiner

Good evening, I just received the attached and have not even looked at it yet but we can schedule a time on Friday to discuss. Are you available the afternoon for a telephone call? Please advise.

Once again, you received the document at 5:44 pm, chose not to review it, and instead sent an email three hours later telling me you did not look at it and asking me to schedule a time to come in and discuss it. Why? There was absolutely no reason I needed to physically visit your "office" when you could have simply forwarded the document and discussed it with me over the phone after you reviewed the response.

This was yet another unnecessary delay—something Rhona had perfected. Her ongoing stalling tactics were more than just frustrating; they were undeniable evidence that she was never truly acting in my best interest. I blame myself for allowing her to treat me so callously. At the time, I was overwhelmed—physically debilitated by recurring shingles outbreaks, mentally worn down from living in a rodent-infested, toxic environment, and emotionally shattered from months of sleepless nights and unbearable stress. My judgment was clouded, and in that state, I didn't see her manipulation for what it was.

GURALNICK & GILLILAND, LLP
ATTORNEYS AT LAW

A FULL SERVICE COMMUNITY
ASSOCIATION LAW FIRM

40-004 COOK STREET, SUITE 3
PALM DESERT, CALIFORNIA 92211
TELEPHONE: (760) 340-1515
FACSIMILE: (760) 568-3053
E-MAIL: WAYNEG@GGHOALAW.COM

PLEASE REFER TO FILE: 84-260

September 14, 2023

EMAIL (Rkauffman@rhonakauffmanlaw.com), FAX (760/406-5095 & 1ST CLASS MAIL
Rhona S. Kauffman, Esq.
Law Offices of Rhona S. Kauffman
Parc Executive Suites - Building A
77564 Country Club Drive, Suite 115
Palm Desert, CA 92211

Re: **Our Client:**   **The Palms Homeowners Association**
       Your Client: **Stephen Steiner, 3155 E. Ramon Road, #808, Palm Springs**
                    ("Subject Unit")
       Subject: **Rodent Infestation**

Dear Ms. Kauffman:

In accordance with our prior communication, this office is corporate counsel to The Palms Homeowners Association ("Association"). The Association has requested that we respond to your August 21, 2023 correspondence regarding the rodent infestation at the Subject Unit.

The Association disagrees with your assertion that it failed in its maintenance and repair obligations but also disagrees as to what those maintenance and repair obligations are. Nevertheless, we will focus on all of the mitigation efforts undertaken by the Association.

PREFERRED PEST CONTROL, WESTERN PHASE 1 AND RODENT BIRD SOLUTION

We enclose various documents and wish to note the following:

1) PREFERRED PEST CONTROL - The Association's pest control vendor is Preferred Pest Control who services the community on a monthly basis. You will note that the first page of the attached document (Preferred Pest Control invoices) references work done at Building 800 which includes the Subject Unit:

- Rodent inspection 11/15/2021
- Screened all openings on roof 11/15/2021

GURALNICK & GILLILAND, LLP.
ATTORNEYS AT LAW

Rhona Kauffman, Esq.
Re: The Palms HOA / Mr. Steiner
Page 2

      - Repaired small stucco voids 11/15/2021
      - Inspected all utility closest areas and screened possible entry areas
      - Installed additional rodent bait stations

      - Rodent inspection 01/11/2022
      - Checked roof and all utility closets
      - Screened additional vent area
      - Checked and re-baited all rodent bait stations
      - Set rodent traps

2) WESTERN EXTERMINATOR COMPANY ("Western") - PART I - Despite the monthly work done by its monthly pest control vendor (including specific attention paid to Building 800), the Association retained Western in November 2022 to perform additional rodent prevention and control at Building 800. You will note the detailed proposal from Western which included inspection, rodent exclusion and eradication and a 3 week intensive rodent trapping program (with traps checked 3 times a week for 3 weeks) and additional bait stations on the exterior of Building 800. Pages 71 - 79 of the Western document are discussed further in the section titled WESTERN PHASE 2 below.

The Association paid Western $3770.00 to perform the work under PHASE 1 detailed in its proposal. It should be further noted that inspections done in May 2023 showed no rodent activity.

3) RODENT BIRD SOLUTION ("RBS") - In addition to Western, the Association also retained RBS in May 2023, at a cost of $1,000.00, to do further rodent exclusion work and set traps in impacted units.

WESTERN PHASE 2

Phase 2 of Western's proposal (Pages 71 -79 of the enclosed document) could not occur until the Association was assured that there was no further rodent activity at the Subject Unit. Phase 2 is to provide a rodent clean and sanitization program of Your Client's attic (as detailed on page 74).

We wish to point out that Your Client did not contact the Association after May 2023 about any further rodent activity. In fact, it was the Association's management that was proactive and contacted Mr. Steiner about completing Phase 2 of Western's proposal. Management was then advised by Mr. Steiner that he had legal counsel and ceased further communications.

The Association has retained Western at a cost of $2,983.00 to perform Phase 2 and just needs Your Client's authorization to facilitate said work at the Subject Unit (but prior to any Phase 2 work,

GURALNICK & GILLILAND, LLP.
ATTORNEYS AT LAW

Rhona Kauffman, Esq.
Re: The Palms HOA / Mr. Steiner
Page 3

please confirm on behalf of Your Client that he is not aware of any current rodent activity related to his Unit).

Please have Mr. Steiner contact Paul Johnson at Seabreeze Management to coordinate Phase 2 of Western's proposal. Mr. Johnson may be reached via phone at (619) 202-1276 or via email at Paul.johnson@seabreezemgmt.com

Do not hesitate to contact the undersigned if you believe additional discussion is warranted.

Sincerely,

Wayne Guralnick

Wayne Guralnick

WG
/mr

Encl.
cc: Association

S:\84-260\Letters\Kauffman.ResponseReRodents.091423.wpd

A SPECIAL PLACE

To begin, I will not dignify the statement "showed no rodent activity" with a detailed response. It is not only patently false but deeply insulting, and it reflects a troubling level of incompetence by opposing counsel.

The HOA's strategy became increasingly clear: shift financial responsibility onto me for a rodent infestation that remained unresolved despite multiple pest control vendors being hired. Each exterminator failed to identify the point of entry—yet because the crawlspace and roof are legally defined as common areas, the costs of those failed efforts were rightfully billed to the HOA, as required under California Civil Code §4775. That statute clearly states that the association—not the homeowner—is responsible for the maintenance, repair, and replacement of common areas, including structural elements that directly affect habitability.

Shockingly, Rhona never once referenced this statute, nor did she assert my rights under the Davis-Stirling Common Interest Development Act—the governing body of law that outlines the duties and obligations of HOAs in California. For an attorney allegedly representing my interests, this omission is not only inexcusable—it is definitive evidence of either gross negligence or a willful attempt to protect the HOA's legal position rather than mine. The fact that she withheld such foundational legal protections—while continuing to delay, stall, and ignore urgent evidence—suggests more than mere incompetence. It strongly implies she was coordinating with or deferring to opposing counsel throughout the process.

Meanwhile, I continued paying $460 a month in HOA dues—payments which explicitly include maintenance of common areas—while living in a hazardous environment the HOA was both legally and ethically obligated to address.

Then came yet another round of pest control—what they called "Phase 2"—as if "Phase 1" had ever yielded a single meaningful result. Rhona was fully aware of the emotional toll this process had taken: repeated visits by exterminators, traps being set in my living space, and no resolution in sight. Rather than providing relief, this new phase appeared to be a calculated attempt to prolong my suffering and drive me further into despair. And I have no doubt that the HOA's legal team understood the financial implications: that resolving the issue properly would be costly. From their perspective, forcing me to abandon my home—or allowing my health to deteriorate—was the cheaper, more convenient solution.

From: Stephen Steiner
To: Rhona S. Kauffman
Subject: FW: Our client: The Palms HOA; Your client: Steiner

SEPTEMBER 14, 2023 / 9:25 PM

I am available. Anytime is good.

From: Stephen Steiner
To: Rhona S. Kauffman
Subject: FW: Our client: The Palms HOA; Your client: Steiner

SEPTEMBER 14, 2023 / 9:27 PM

BTW, the rats are all back. They went crazy in the kitchen when I toasted up a pop-tart.

From: Stephen Steiner
To: Rhona S. Kauffman
Subject: FW: Our client: The Palms HOA; Your client: Steiner

SEPTEMBER 15, 2023 / 1:42 AM

Rats were active so took video holding infrared device. You can hear the rats and see how disgusting it is.

From: Stephen Steiner
To: Rhona S. Kauffman
Subject: Re: FW: Our client: The Palms HOA; Your client: Steiner

SEPTEMBER 15, 2023 / 11:54 AM

Got zero sleep. I am attaching a video from last night of the activity. At the three minute mark you can hear them running around the kitchen crawlspace. I also shot the video with my thermal reader in front of the camera so you can see what the rats have done. I went through the entire condo so it is about 9 mins.

I read the lawyers response and once again I am not shocked but angry. I asked the last exterminator who came to my condo when they find the entry point and get this all repaired. His answer was he didn't know if they would find the opening or what else they can do.

For the HOA and Seabreeze to say I did not contact them after May 23 is complete stupidity. Western Exterminators failed to return on a weekly basis or call me to see if the rodent activity has stopped. The last exterminator (the one that said he had no clue how to solve this situation) also told me that when the heat inside the crawlspace gets over 86° the rats will not return.

Apparently the rats cannot live in temperatures over 86°, they will die. At that time temperatures were over 100° and the rat activity was tapering off. He knew this and so during the summer there were only a few times when a rat entered the crawlspace.

Having the lawyer show the expenses for the exterminators is insulting. I have suffered mental and physical stress for almost two years. My life was completely turned upside down. I had to go on medication for mental stress. My shingles were so bad that I wished I was dead. I had to go to the ER because of a skin fungus.

They destroyed me for what reason? Are they getting a big bonus for saving money by avoiding what they legally have to repair. Making a new hole in my ceiling and sending exterminators over three times a week, dragging it out month after month till I go completely insane and die.

Is this their solution to avoid replacing my entire ceiling? It is their job to help me. That is what the HOA and Seabreeze are there for. For the Homeowner.

Instead, they made me out to be the problem because Donna did not do her job. If this was Donna's condo I guarantee this would have been resolved immediately along with the repairs.

I am living in a toxic environment. It is their job to fix this. Look at the video. My entire condo is toxic. I will go to court over this. There is no reason they should fight me on this. I am a human being. You do not treat another human like this. Ask any of them if they would like to switch homes with me. I will be very happy too. Did they look a the "Rat Exclusion Plan"?

I had to purchase three air purifiers that run all day. I don't use my kitchen. I get no sleep. I clean constantly. Do they honestly think that if this goes to court they will win? This is exactly what a Slum Lord would do.

That is my rant. I am so exhausted from this. I don't think I can take not sleeping for days anymore. They need to rent a house and move me out until it is safe to return.

Here is a link to the video.

Thank you for all your help with this. I appreciate it greatly.

From: Rhona S. Kauffman
To: Stephen Steiner
Subject: Re: Our client The Palms HOA Your client Steiner

SEPTEMBER 15, 2023 / 12:08 PM

With your permission, I will forward that email to Guralnick & Gilliland

---

From: Rhona S. Kauffman
To: Stephen Steiner
Subject: Re: Our client The Palms HOA Your client Steiner

SEPTEMBER 15, 2023 / 12:08 PM

I tried to open the attachment on my phone, but it doesn't open without passwords, and it won't be able to be a forward it. Can you send it in a different format?

Rhona's level of incompetence was astonishing. I am absolutely certain the file opened—she had the latest iPhone, and the format I used was compatible with virtually any device. Her claim that she couldn't open it was nothing more than a flimsy excuse. It was a deliberate attempt to manufacture confusion and, more importantly, to avoid forwarding critical evidence — evidence that clearly documented the severity of the infestation—to the opposing counsel.

From: Stephen Steiner
To: Rhona S. Kauffman
Subject: Re: Our client The Palms HOA Your client Steiner

SEPTEMBER 15, 2023 / 12:10 PM

Please do.

A SPECIAL PLACE

From: Stephen Steiner
To: Rhona S. Kauffman
Subject: Re: Our client The Palms HOA Your client Steiner

SEPTEMBER 15, 2023 / 12:22 PM

Shared from my google drive.

From: Rhona S. Kauffman
To: Stephen Steiner
Subject: Re: Our client The Palms HOA Your client Steiner

SEPTEMBER 17, 2023 / 2:22 PM

Stephen I cannot forward since it is not in the right format. If you can attach the video and email to me then I can open look at it and forward to HOA counsel.

If you were unable—or unwilling—to view the evidence yourself, the appropriate course of action would have been to forward my email directly to opposing counsel. Failing to do so demonstrates either a lack of basic competence or a deliberate effort to obstruct the submission of critical evidence.

From: Stephen Steiner
To: Rhona S. Kauffman
Subject: Re: Our client The Palms HOA Your client Steiner

SEPTEMBER 17, 2023 / 10:15 PM

If they believe there are no more rats then when are they going to do the clean up? Donna said they would and I want the cleanup done so I can sell.

From: Stephen Steiner
To: Rhona S. Kauffman
Subject: Re: Our client The Palms HOA Your client Steiner

SEPTEMBER 17, 2023 / 10:42 PM

Send this link to them. I put all videos on my site.

From: Rhona S. Kauffman
To: Stephen Steiner
Subject: Re: Our client The Palms HOA Your client Steiner

SEPTEMBER 17, 2023 / 10:45 PM

Please note that is not sufficient as it shows no rats or any time stamp. We are trying to prove that rats are still invading your ceiling. I had asked you to get a new company to come over who was not ever previously involved and also you are not to tell them about any of the prior companies. They can do a report documenting the current problems.

Do you have any videos that you can just send as an attachment wherein I can represent that they were taken within the past couple days and they show the rats with time stamp would be perfect and of course I need that report above to send as well.

From: Stephen Steiner
To: Rhona S. Kauffman
Subject: Re: Our client The Palms HOA Your client Steiner

SEPTEMBER 17, 2023 / 10:50 PM

The one that I took with the infrared was taken on the 14th but only the time was on that. I will just have to shoot more video.

From: Stephen Steiner
To: Rhona S. Kauffman
Subject: Re: Our client The Palms HOA Your client Steiner

SEPTEMBER 18, 2023 / 12:22 AM

They need to repair the three holes made in my ceiling. I don't care anymore about this place. This is a stupid game they are playing and I always lose. When they do the repairs I will sell and they can all rejoice in their win. I will let the new owners deal with this.

A SPECIAL PLACE

From: Rhona S. Kauffman
  To: Stephen Steiner
Subject: Re: Our client The Palms HOA Your client Steiner

SEPTEMBER 18, 2023 / 8:03 AM

You are right and I believe you. We just need to show them. How can I help?

From: Stephen Steiner
  To: Rhona S. Kauffman
Subject: Re: Our client The Palms HOA Your client Steiner

SEPTEMBER 18, 2023 / 8:29 AM

Well last night was another active night. I know how to show them. I ordered a borescope inspection cam. It is very small and has an led at the head of it. It is used to check down pipes. I will position it where all the activity is. If it works well I will order two more and have an enormous amount of footage.

From: Stephen Steiner
  To: Rhona S. Kauffman
Subject: Code Compliance

SEPTEMBER 26, 2023 / 5:46 PM

I am having Code Compliance come out and evaluate the condition of my condo. I want to see what they have to say about my living conditions. I got my endoscope so I will be taking video too.

From: Stephen Steiner
  To: Rhona S. Kauffman
Subject: For Your Records

SEPTEMBER 28, 2023 / 9:08 PM

Been getting maggots last couple of days, and today, it looks like a rat has been trying to get into the laundry area. Left a mess on the dryer.

Due to the placement of traps directly above the washer and dryer, rodents that died in the crawlspace were left to decay in that area. As their bodies decomposed, maggots developed and eventually began falling through the ceiling light fixtures into my living space. The security camera wire—which passed through a small hole directly above the dryer—became a target for rodents attempting to gnaw their way into the interior of the condo, further exacerbating the health hazard.

The aftermath of this unsanitary situation was horrifying. Large horse flies, hatched from the maggots, filled the unit—forcing me to spend my days swatting them in an effort to maintain some degree of cleanliness and sanity. The constant stress, stench, and infestation made it feel as though I were living in a nightmare—a real-life version of the Amityville Horror. This was not simply a pest control issue; it was a sustained assault on my mental and physical health, allowed to persist through the gross negligence of the HOA, Seabreeze Management, and all involved.

Mo	Tu	We	Th	Fr	Sa	Su
						~~1~~
~~2~~	~~3~~	~~4~~	~~5~~	~~6~~	~~7~~	~~8~~
~~9~~	10	11	~~12~~	13	14	15
16	17	~~18~~	~~19~~	20	~~21~~	22
~~23~~	24	~~25~~	~~26~~	~~27~~	28	29
30	~~31~~					

OCTOBER

475 DAYS
UNRESOLVED

A SPECIAL PLACE

From: Stephen Steiner
To: Rhona S. Kauffman
Subject: Condo

OCTOBER 11, 2023 / 7:39 PM

My house is filled with giant flies, so I have decided to sell. I am sick of dealing with the stupidity and cruelty they are subjecting me to. They are disgusting human beings. From the beginning, their goal was to do the least amount of work and destroy me personally. I have endured an enormous amount of depression and stress because of their incompetence.

The Palms has become a prison to me. It was my last connection to my partner and our life together. Donna and Shelley destroyed what great memories I had. I hope they understand the damage they have done.

Before I go completely broke, I am going to end this pointless fight, which they know they are responsible for fixing. I guarantee the entire 800 building is filled with rats. I tried to get exterminators and the city to come out, but it was like I was blacklisted.

As far as life goes, most of the time, I wish I never existed. Living on a planet with humans that treat other humans this way makes life pointless. I can never find anyone that will do the right thing. They should have done everything possible to fix this. They did the exact opposite. I hope they are happy and proud of what they did.

I would prefer to not let them know I am selling until it is listed. Knowing how they operate, they will cause issues. I will cover the cost to repair all the holes Donna had the exterminators cut into my ceiling. I would like to end our contract as soon as it sells.

From: Rhona S. Kauffman
To: Stephen Steiner
Subject: RE: Condo

OCTOBER 11, 2023 / 9:23 PM

I would like to talk to you about it. Can we speak this week?

After pouring my heart out in a deeply personal and distressing email—describing not just the physical horrors I endured in my home, but the psychological toll it had taken on my life—Rhona's only reply was, "I would like to talk to you about it. Can we speak this week?" A vague, indifferent response that showed no urgency, no empathy, and no recognition of the seriousness of what I was going through.

At that point, I had made it abundantly clear: I was surrounded by filth, plagued by giant flies, grieving the emotional loss of a home that once symbolized love and partnership, and teetering on the edge of financial and emotional collapse. And yet, her reply read like a generic calendar appointment. No action plan. No validation. No acknowledgment of the trauma I had endured.

It was as if none of what I had written mattered. As if she hadn't read it at all—or worse, read it and chose to respond as though it were a routine inquiry rather than a desperate cry for help. Her detached response spoke volumes. It confirmed what I had long suspected: I was not her client in any meaningful sense. I was a burden—someone to pacify, delay, and ultimately dismiss.

This moment encapsulated the entire experience. I wasn't just failed by my attorney. I was failed by someone who had a legal and ethical obligation to fight for me. Instead, she mirrored the same apathy and cruelty I had faced from the HOA and Seabreeze Management. And by doing so, she became part of the harm.

From: Stephen Steiner
To: Rhona S. Kauffman
Subject: RE: Condo

OCTOBER 12, 2023 / 8:51 PM

Anytime you want. I am home with the flies and rats.

They are doing exactly what they did when I notified them about the rats. All they do is drag it out until I can't take it anymore. The city won't do anything. The last time Donna intervened and told them she took care of it. It was all because I blind copied the CEO of Seabreeze and she retaliated. The one thing Donna did tell me was that everything above the ceiling is HOA and they would clean it up. All lies.

She told the exterminators to do the minimum. The owner of Western Exterminators came over with one of his employees who came three times a week to check the traps. He told me they would spray the crawlspace with a chemical that would sanitize it. I called BS on that, and his employee, from the look on his face, knew it was BS. I also told him that all the insulation needed to be replaced because it was soaked with urine and a lot of it had been pulled down. He said it was the building settling that caused the insulation to fall. Again, I called BS, and the employee rolled his eyes. After that meeting, I did not see the employee again and was told he found another job.

All this drama for rats. I can't believe they are going to all this insanity. I pay $460 a month for what? I guarantee if I could get an exterminator from another city to come out and do a full inspection, this entire building would be red-tagged.

The neighbor below has his unit on the market, and so does my neighbor. I know that as soon as this is all exposed, the value of the condos will drop, and they will not sell. As usual, I am the one who is the troublemaker. The HOA has done everything to keep this covered up. Only a few people in the complex know about the rat problem, but they don't seem to care or were told it was taken care of. It is never mentioned at the HOA meetings that I no longer attend after they praised Donna on all the excellent work she did and promoted her to a new development to manage.

I know HOAs have a lot of power and can, as they already have, make my life miserable. It seems that everyone in Palm Springs is against me. I used to be a happy person, but they turned me into what I am now.

Let me know when is good for you to talk. Sorry for the long email.

From: Rhona S. Kauffman
To: Stephen Steiner
Subject: RE: Condo

OCTOBER 12, 2023 / 11:18 PM

Let's set up a time on Monday to talk on the telephone unless you want to meet at my office on Tuesday.

Why not discuss this now, rather than waste more time arranging yet another in-person meeting at your 'office'? These unnecessary delays have become a consistent pattern in your handling of my case, and I see no justification for continuing them.

From: Stephen Steiner
To: Rhona S. Kauffman
Subject: I WANT YOU TO SUE THEM

OCTOBER 13, 2023 / 7:24 AM

Once again, RATS!

There is another rat running around the crawlspace. I don't know what to do. Please, please, please sue them. I am literally going insane. I get no sleep. I spent two days trying to kill all the flies.

PLEASE SUE THEM. I can't take it anymore. I want to kill myself to stop the suffering. I don't care that everyone thinks I am nuts. PLEASE DO SOMETHING. I DON'T WANT TO LIVE THIS WAY ANYMORE. I NEED HELP. NO ONE IS LISTENING TO ME. PLEASE, PLEASE, PLEASE.

Rhona, as my retained legal counsel, your duty is to act in accordance with my instructions and represent my interests zealously. When a client directs their attorney to initiate legal action, it is your professional obligation to proceed—not to delay or deflect. I retained your services to advocate on my behalf, yet to date, you have taken no meaningful action. Your continued inaction is not only unacceptable—it constitutes a fundamental failure in your responsibility as my legal representative.

From: Stephen Steiner
To: Rhona S. Kauffman
Subject: RE: Condo

OCTOBER 13, 2023 / 7:39 AM

I want you to come to my condo today so you can experience what I do. No more office visits and no more discussing it. I don't want to live like this anymore. I am literally going nuts. It has been over a year and a half living like this and everyone is ignoring me and acting like I am making this up. I am tired of dealing with this. Do I have to die for something to be done?

Why are they not fixing this? There is a ton of evidence. The condo is infested with rats. I got sick from it. Why is the HOA and Seabreeze not fixing this? What do I have to do to get people to listen to me? Do I have to act like a lunatic, scream outside, smash everything? Please tell me. NO ONE IS LISTENING TO ME. EVERYONE IGNORES THE ISSUE AND ME. PLEASE FILE A LAWSUIT.

SEND AN EXTERMINATOR. I cannot go through the smell of another dead rat and all the flies. Day after day after day. This is all Shelley and Donna's fault. They did nothing. They dragged it out hoping this would happen to me, and it has.

I want to live a quiet life and I can't. Please do something. It is a nightmare here. Just look at the thermal image video. Who gives a shit about a date stamp? Have the HOA come over and I will personally give them a live view. Would anyone of them live knowing all that is up above their heads?

I didn't do anything wrong. Why are they doing this to me?

PLEASE HELP.

It is important to note that from the very beginning of our professional relationship, Rhona made no effort whatsoever to visit my condo and assess, first-hand, the hazardous and toxic conditions I was forced to endure. On multiple occasions, I urged her to come to the property to witness the severity of the infestation and the uninhabitable state of the unit. Instead of responding appropriately, she routinely deflected, changed the subject, or resorted to dismissive and demeaning language—at times accusing me of exaggerating or being the cause of my own circumstances. Such conduct was not only unprofessional but demonstrated a blatant disregard for her client's health, wellbeing, and the integrity of the case.

From: Stephen Steiner
To: Rhona S. Kauffman
Subject: Update

OCTOBER 13, 2023 / 1:47 PM

I want to make sure that something is sent to them today. I do not want to wait any longer. May 23 is when I had the consultation, and August 21 is when they received the demand. I need this to move quickly before I go completely nuts. They have had plenty of time to fix this. I do not want to wait anymore.

They are not interested in mediation from the response given on the demand. I don't want mediation. Tell them I do not care to mediate this since they already know the problem and refused to fix it.

Everyone ignores me. I am done with that. Sue them. They will drag this out forever. Even with mediation, they will still drag it out. I don't want to live in this condo anymore. They need to pay for a place for me to live since this is all their fault.

From: Stephen Steiner
To: Cam Kjeldgaard
Subject: Re: This is Cam

OCTOBER 13, 2023 / 7:07 PM

You remembered!!

Here is the video. It's a wonderful place to live. You can thank Donna and Shelley for doing nothing.

From: Stephen Steiner
To: Cam Kjeldgaard
Subject: Re: This is Cam

OCTOBER 13, 2023 / 7:09 PM

If you want, I can come and check your ceiling. I am curious to see if they got into yours too.

From: Stephen Steiner
To: Cam Kjeldgaard
Subject: Re: This is Cam

OCTOBER 13, 2023 / 7:16 PM

You can also see where there is no insulation. All the black circles are insulation soaked with urine and poop. At the 3-minute mark, you can see how much urine has run down the wall in the second bedroom.

But according to them, there are no rats.

Cam, my downstairs neighbor, was a part-time resident—what many refer to as a snowbird—who only stayed in Palm Springs during the winter months. I had shared the thermal imaging video and asked if he would like to see if his condo was affected by any rodent activity. Given that his condo was on the ground floor and the crawlspace above it was virtually nonexistent, it was unaffected.

A SPECIAL PLACE

From: Rhona S. Kauffman
To: Stephen Steiner
Subject: Re: Condo

OCTOBER 13, 2023 / 10:00 AM

Stephen, let's move forward and demand mediation. This is ridiculous. You should not be living this way. And then we can file a complaint if mediation does not work.

I understand the rats are still there. I know I asked you for a report from a current unrelated pest company. Did you ever get that report?

Despite having hired Rhona to represent me, her complete lack of urgency was alarming and deeply inappropriate. As my legal counsel, it was her responsibility—not mine—to arrange for a qualified exterminator to inspect the property and document the uninhabitable conditions I was living in. Instead, she continually pushed that burden onto me, forcing me to do the legwork that she should have taken initiative on as part of building my case.

Adding to my frustration, nearly every extermination company I contacted personally would place me on hold as soon as I gave them my address. Without exception, they would then tell me they would call back—yet none ever did. It was as though I had been blacklisted. This disturbing pattern strongly suggested outside interference and left me even more isolated in trying to obtain help.

Eventually, I located a company willing to send someone out. Within two minutes of arriving, the technician identified the source of the infestation: a rat had chewed through the garbage disposal pipe inside the wall, using it as a pathway to travel into the ceiling. This perfectly explained the persistent stench near the sink and why a nest had formed above it. The technician informed me he would file a written report and that I could call their office and speak with Gloria to have it emailed to me.

When I followed up an hour later, my call went to voicemail. I left a message—then another, every day for a week. I finally reached the company owner, who claimed the team had been on vacation and reassured me that Gloria would send the report. But when I got through to her, she placed me on hold, then returned and said flatly, "I'm sorry, there is no report."

I was stunned. I reminded her that the exterminator had been to my condo and promised to file documentation. She replied that while he had visited, he "did not find any rodents," and therefore, no report was generated. I explained that this documentation was crucial for pending legal action, but she refused to provide anything further.

This deliberate runaround, coupled with Rhona's failure to advocate on my behalf or take control of the process, left me to manage tasks that were clearly within her scope of duty. Her indifference and repeated failure to act not only undermined my case but added to the emotional and psychological distress I was already experiencing from living in a toxic, rodent-infested environment.

From: Stephen Steiner
To: Rhona S. Kauffman
Subject: Lawsuit

OCTOBER 13, 2023 / 10:03 AM

I have been dealing with this since July 2022. I want to sue them for $3M—$100,000 for each month (15 x $100,000) and double it because of the response the lawyers gave. Every month that goes by, increase it by $200,000. I am suffering because of them.

Please make sure Shelley and Donna are included in the lawsuit. They are well aware of all of this and did nothing but accuse me.

I now have a rash and shingles. I have to go through this nightmare again.

Please have them send their exterminator since they think I am making it all up. Maybe he can shoot video with a date and time stamp.

They must remove the infestation. It is their responsibility.

They will also need to rent a home of equal or greater value until the cleanup is done.

From: Stephen Steiner
To: Rhona S. Kauffman
Subject: Re: Condo

OCTOBER 13, 2023 / 10:09 AM

I called two of them and neither responded. I will call all of the exterminators until someone comes here.

Last night was a nightmare, and I apologize for the emails. I panic every time I have to open a cabinet or door. When I heard the rat, I couldn't take it anymore. I am living in my guest room because of the HOA and Seabreeze.

I will keep you posted on the exterminator.

From: Rhona S. Kauffman
To: Stephen Steiner
Subject: Re: Condo

OCTOBER 13, 2023 / 10:13 AM

Don't apologize. It's understandable, but it's time to do something about it

It's 'time to do something about it'? Rhona, I retained your services in May for that exact purpose. You were hired to take action—immediate and decisive action—not to stall, deflect, or perpetuate the same delays already inflicted by the HOA and Seabreeze Management. Your failure to act in a timely and competent manner has directly contributed to the prolonged suffering I've endured. It is abundantly clear that your inaction was not incidental, but intentional. These repeated delays served no one but the opposing party, raising serious questions about where your true allegiances lie.

From: Stephen Steiner
To: Rhona S. Kauffman
Subject: Re: Condo

OCTOBER 13, 2023 / 10:17 AM

Seems like everyone is selling because they know this is going to be red-tagged. If you get a chance to view the video, you will see how bad it is. There is urine flowing all down the wall in my guest room.

I have to stay in that room because it has no access points. This is the life I live. I wish they were forced to live here.

From: Stephen Steiner
To: Rhona S. Kauffman
Subject: Re: Condo

OCTOBER 13, 2023 / 10:19 AM

If they agree to mediation, they either accept all my demands or we take this to court. They need to pay for what they did to me.

From: Stephen Steiner
To: Rhona S. Kauffman
Subject: Exterminator

OCTOBER 13, 2023 / 10:36 AM

Called one that actually answered, and they said they cannot take the job because of the situation. I am assuming most will not take it because of the HOA. I am sure it is something the HOA deals with and not the homeowner. Not sure what to do. I am sure they all will turn me down.

From: Stephen Steiner
To: Rhona S. Kauffman
Subject: Exterminators

OCTOBER 13, 2023 / 10:55 AM

No one will come out. HOA has to approve it.

Shelley (who does not live here or in this state) has to have the board approve.

I don't want to do mediation. They had their chance, and they blew it. File the lawsuit. I don't want to hear their lame excuses and deal with exterminators coming in and out over and over while they don't solve the problem.

No mediation. I know it is how it is done, but I refuse.

From: Rhona S. Kauffman
To: Stephen Steiner
Subject: Re: Exterminator

OCTOBER 13, 2023 / 11:09 AM

How did they know about the situation? You didn't mention it, right?

A SPECIAL PLACE

From: Stephen Steiner
   To: Rhona S. Kauffman
Subject: Re: Exterminator

OCTOBER 13, 2023 / 11:14 AM

They know because it is a condo. They always ask. Normally, I would contact Seabreeze, and they would send out the exterminator. That is why nobody returns my calls. They ask for the address and then put me on hold. Either they never call back, or they tell me they cannot do it.

From: Stephen Steiner
   To: Rhona S. Kauffman
Subject: Exterminator

OCTOBER 13, 2023 / 11:17 AM

Unless it is done by the HOA, they will void everything and hold me responsible for the cleanup.

From: Stephen Steiner
   To: Rhona S. Kauffman
Subject: Latest News

OCTOBER 14, 2023 / 7:09 AM

Not sure where everything stands with this case and if they intend to do anything.

Three days ago, the mother rat had her babies in the crawlspace above the kitchen.

I have attached a video clip (with time and date stamp) you can forward to their lawyers. You can clearly hear the babies squealing and the mother rustling around. This happens all day.

They are welcome to come over or send an exterminator to confirm. I will not allow them to make another opening to kill them. I have gone through enough of their games to delay. If you feel this is a losing battle, please let me know, and I will leave the rats to live in the crawlspace and sell.

At this point, mediation is pointless. I don't really know what mediation would do. I want the rats gone and everything cleaned up. I will not accept anything else.

How this is not against the law is baffling to me.

From: Stephen Steiner
   To: Rhona S. Kauffman
Subject: RE: Condo

OCTOBER 14, 2023 / 7:41 AM

Here is the video. If you are unable to view it, send it to someone in your office or text it to your phone. It will open there.

From: Stephen Steiner
   To: Rhona S. Kauffman
Subject: Hi

OCTOBER 14, 2023 / 8:54 AM

First, I want to apologize for all the crazy emails. The stress from all the flies and the rat running around in the crawlspace, the lack of sleep, and the smell drove me over the edge.

It has been almost two years of this, and their lack of empathy for my situation makes me very angry. Even my neighbors turn a blind eye.

I watched a video on YouTube about HOAs, and apparently, they have all the power. I need your honest opinion. Is this worth pursuing? If not, I will have all the holes patched, do a little touch-up, and put it on the market.

I want this over, and after watching the video, the HOA can do just about anything they want, and I have no power to stop it.

I will let the new tenant deal with the rats and the cleanup… which will never happen.

Sorry again for the psychotic episode.

From: Rhona S. Kauffman
To: Stephen SteineR
Subject: Re: Latest News

Can I call you at one today?

From: Stephen Steiner
To: Rhona S. Kauffman
Subject: Re: Latest News

Yes.

From: Rhona S. Kauffman
To: Stephen Steiner
Subject: FW: Our client: The Palms HOA; Your client: Steiner

Forwarding response and documentation regarding The Palms HOA from Guralnick & Gilliland, LLP.

Had Rhona demonstrated even a minimal level of investment in my case, she would have known that she had already sent the response and accompanying documentation back on September 14th. Her failure to recall such a critical action only underscores her lack of engagement and attention to detail in representing my interests.

From: Stephen Steiner
To: Rhona S. Kauffman
Subject: Response to Documents

Upon carefully reviewing the documents, I recall going through them. Our initial plan was to set up a meeting to discuss these documents. However, we got sidetracked when I shared a video of the rats, and it was pointed out that there was no timestamp on it.

The proposal from Rodent and Bird Solution essentially mirrors what all the other exterminators have offered, except for the smoke test. Implementing the smoke test would require tenant involvement, which, given the current situation with two units up for sale, would be highly impractical.

I'm opposed to the idea of exterminators setting traps or visiting my condo multiple times a week for inspections. This approach only prolongs the issue without providing a genuine solution.

Based on my observations, it seems likely that the rats are entering through a hole under the roof tiles. I used a thermal imaging camera, which clearly shows where they've built nests beneath the roof.

I've reached out to a few contractors and am currently awaiting their responses.

From: Jennifer Curlowicz
To: Stephen Steiner
Cc: Orlando Peters
Subject: Submission form to DeWolf Construction & Renovations

I received your submission to discuss your construction project. When is a good time to call you?

If you prefer, you can also reach out to me.

I would love to discuss your project needs with you.

Respectfully,

Jennifer Peters, Administration
DeWolf Construction & Renovations

In an effort to expose the extent of the damage caused by the ongoing rodent infestation, I contacted a construction company to request an estimate for a kitchen remodel. My intention was to use the remodeling process to reveal the hidden contamination and structural impact, thereby providing undeniable proof that the infestation remained unresolved and that proper remediation would require substantial cleanup. At the time, I believed this would be the breakthrough needed to compel action.

From: Rhona S. Kauffman
  To: Stephen Steiner
Subject: RE: Latest News

Stephen, can I call you tomorrow at a time convenient for you, or are you finding a contractor?

From: Stephen Steiner
  To: Rhona S. Kauffman
Subject: RE: Latest News

I actually did find one. They will be coming out next week on Tuesday. I am waiting on another to get back to me as a backup in case the first bails. Hopefully, I will know tonight or in the morning.

From: Stephen Steiner
  To: Jennifer Curlowicz
Subject: Re: Submission form to DeWolf Construction & Renovations

Here is a thermal video of what it looks like in the crawlspace. I get to live with this every day.

In hindsight, my critical misstep was disclosing the extent of the rodent damage and sharing the thermal imaging video. That information, intended to prompt urgent action, was instead used against me.

From: Stephen Steiner
  To: Jennifer Curlowicz
Subject: Re: Submission form to DeWolf Construction & Renovations

Checking in to see if your contractor will be coming today.

Please let me know as soon as possible.

From: Jennifer Peters
  To: Stephen Steiner
Subject: Re: Submission form to DeWolf Construction & Renovations

Sorry it took so long to get back to you. We have been dealing with an emergency. We are not in a position to take your project at this time and will have to politely decline.

From: Stephen Steiner
  To: Rhona S. Kauffman
Subject: Another strike out

Not sure why, but both canceled. I will keep calling others. Today was an extremely smelly day. I guess another rat died and is rotting.

I find it strange that not one of them has come to my condo to see what I live in. If they think I am lying, then they should come over.

Is there a reason the HOA and Seabreeze are treating my situation like I am the problem?

From: Rhona S. Kauffman
  To: Stephen Steiner
Subject: Re: Another strike out

Maybe I should find someone for you. Would you like that?

Rhona, I hired you to represent me and protect my interests. Instead, you've consistently failed to act, dismissed my concerns, and spoken to me in a demeaning and condescending manner.

	Mo	Tu	We	Th	Fr	Sa	Su
					~~1~~	~~2~~	~~3~~
	~~4~~	~~5~~	~~6~~	~~7~~	~~8~~	~~9~~	~~10~~
	~~11~~	~~12~~	~~13~~	~~14~~	~~15~~	~~16~~	~~17~~
	~~18~~	~~19~~	~~20~~	~~21~~	~~22~~	~~23~~	~~24~~
	~~25~~	~~26~~	~~27~~	~~28~~	~~29~~	~~30~~	

NOVEMBER

505 DAYS UNRESOLVED

A SPECIAL PLACE

From: Stephen Steiner
To: Erik Newman
Subject: Mouse

NOVEMBER 1, 2023 / 5:41 AM

I hear a mouse running around my attic/crawlspace. Need to get someone out here to give me a quote to remove and make sure others do not follow.

Please give me a call.

From: Erik Newman
To: Stephen Steiner
Subject: Re: Mouse

NOVEMBER 1, 2023 / 12:29 PM

Please give my office a call to schedule.

From: Stephen Steiner
To: Erik Newman
Subject: Re: Mouse

NOVEMBER 2, 2023 / 11:05 AM

Left a message on that number.

From: Erik Newman
To: Stephen Steiner
Subject: Re: Mouse

NOVEMBER 2, 2023 / 5:25 PM

Great, thanks.

From: Stephen Steiner
To: Rhona S. Kauffman
Subject: Finally

NOVEMBER 6, 2023 / 1:14 PM

I finally got an exterminator to come over who found where the rats are getting into my place - turns out it's a pipe in the kitchen. I should have realized it because I often heard rat noises there.

The exterminator also mentioned that my living conditions are really bad and I should not be living in the condo because it is toxic. He said the ceiling, walls, and insulation all need to be replaced. He'll be sending me a detailed report later today, which I'll email to you. He also suggested getting Code Enforcement involved.

Once I have the report, I'll take it to Code Enforcement. The HOA and Seabreeze will cover the cost of everything, and I want compensation for almost two years of suffering in this disgusting environment. The exterminator said traditional rat traps wouldn't have solved this issue. Funny how he found the entry point in one minute, and all the others never found it.

I would love to see what their lawyers say. Please let them know they are welcome to come stay the night at my place and enjoy what they created.

I would love for this to go to court so I can see their faces when they lose this case and compensate me for two long painful years of pain, suffering, and defamation.

From: Rhona S. Kauffman
To: Stephen Steiner
Subject: Re: FINALLY!

NOVEMBER 6, 2023 / 6:03 PM

Perfect, get me the report so I can survey response letter to the law firm.

From: Stephen Steiner
To: Rhona S. Kauffman
Subject: Re: FINALLY!

NOVEMBER 6, 2023 / 9:52 PM

Will do, he said today but looks like tomorrow.

From: Stephen Steiner
To: Erik Newman
Subject: Question

Thanks for getting one of you staff "forgot his name-sorry" out here. He was awesome and found the point of entry in under a minute.

Here is my question.

How was your employee able to find the entry point within a minute when Western Exterminators and Preferred Pest Control could not find it and gave up after almost 2 years? You think they would eventually figure it out in a month or two.

Western and Preferred have been to my condo countless times (at one point I had someone come three times a week) during that time period. The owner of Western was in my condo while two of his staff made a new entry point in the master bedroom closet ceiling, which is farthest from the kitchen. I would think of all people he would have known immediately where they were entering.

I am getting the feeling my HOA and Seabreeze Management purposely made me suffer for two years because I reported them to Code Enforcement. I have been very sick many times over the past years and they did nothing but send exterminators to make more holes in my ceiling and place traps delaying the clean up. They were not concerned that a homeowner was living in conditions that the city would most likely red tag.

I think my HOA pulled revenge on me. Western and Preferred most likely knew exactly how and where the rats were entering.

Please send the report over as soon as possible so I can forward to my attorney.

Enjoy a thermal imaging video of my ceiling. I live below it 24/7.

Thanks again. Finally someone believes me.

From: Stephen Steiner
To: Rhona S. Kauffman
Subject: Question

Quick question.

How did Newman Termite and Pest Control find the entry point within a minute when Western Exterminators and Preferred Pest Control could not find it and gave up after a year and a half?

I am getting the feeling that Shelley and Donna purposely made me suffer for two years because I reported them to Code Enforcement.

Is that possible? Donna and Shelley were very mad and sent that ridiculous email claiming "incredible and extraordinary" steps they took to resolve the situation.

Something seems off and I feel like this was all done out of revenge. They never planned on resolving the situation.

What do you think?

Sent an email to Erik Newman for the report this morning. I will send it the second I get it.

From: Stephen Steiner
To: Rhona S. Kauffman
Subject: Re: Question

Called, emailed, left messages… it's as if I don't exist. I'll wait till tomorrow and call another exterminator outside this valley.

How anyone gets anything done here is a mystery to me.

From: Rhona S. Kauffman
To: Stephen Steiner
Subject: Re: Question

NOVEMBER 7, 2023 / 10:47 AM

Yes, and it goes to your complaint, so get me that report.

From: Stephen Steiner
To: Erik Newman
Subject: Inspection report

NOVEMBER 8, 2023 / 4:08 PM

Can you please email me the inspection report for 3155 E Ramon Rd, Unit 808?

I was told it would be sent later that evening, and two days have passed.

If there is some issue, please let me know so I can find another exterminator.

From: Stephen Steiner
To: Rhona S. Kauffman
Subject: Re: Question

NOVEMBER 9, 2023 / 9:16 AM

I called and emailed the owner Erik Newman for the report. No response.

The exterminator that came over did mention they service several of the condos in this complex. He had the code to get into the property without me buzzing him in. So this is probably why they are ghosting me. They must have gotten a heads-up or they realize how bad it is and are avoiding getting involved for fear they will lose business.

I will try again to get another exterminator.

All this drama over roof rats.

From: Rhona S. Kauffman
To: Stephen Steiner
Subject: Re: Question

NOVEMBER 9, 2023 / 11:22 AM

I remember a contractor may be able to do something or say something to you in a report.

From: Rhona S. Kauffman
To: Stephen Steiner
Subject: Re: Question

NOVEMBER 9, 2023 / 11:22 AM

You need to get someone from far away out of the area.

From: Stephen Steiner
To: Rhona S. Kauffman
Subject: Re: Question

NOVEMBER 9, 2023 / 1:08 PM

I had a contractor who was going to come out but sent this response a few days later:

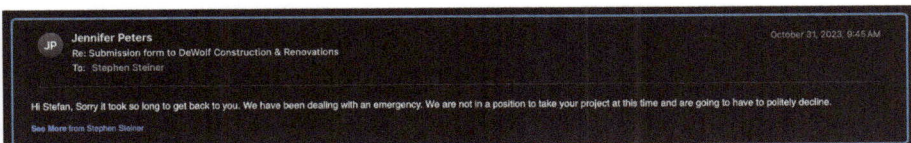

> **Jennifer Peters**
> Re: Submission form to DeWolf Construction & Renovations
> To: Stephen Steiner
>
> *October 31, 2023, 9:45 AM*
>
> Hi Stefan, Sorry it took so long to get back to you. We have been dealing with an emergency. We are not in a position to take your project at this time and are going to have to politely decline.
>
> See More from Stephen Steiner

Of course, they got my name wrong. This is turning into the Da Vinci Code.

It was particularly suspicious that Jennifer Peters misspelled my name—despite it being clearly visible in the 'To:' line of the email. This mirrored the same pattern of carelessness I experienced with Rhona, who repeatedly did the same. The similarities in their behavior raise serious concerns that they may have been in communication with one another, and that these actions were not coincidental, but potentially a subtle and unprofessional form of mockery.

From: Erik Newman
To: Stephen Steiner
Subject: Re: Question

I'm glad to hear my tech was able to find another entry point. We're not positive that the entry point is the only location of how they are getting in, but I hope this solves your problem.

I'm currently on vacation, but my office will send you the report. If you have any further questions, please contact my office.

From: Erik Newman
To: Stephen Steiner
Subject: Re: Inspection report

NOVEMBER 9, 2023 / *5:07 PM*

Sorry Stephen, I'm on vacation. Please contact my office at **760-250-6422** if you haven't received it already. My office should be able to send it right over.

From: Rhona S. Kauffman
To: Stephen Steiner
Subject: RE: Question

NOVEMBER 9, 2023 / *5:15 PM*

Is he the guy who told you the rats are present?

From: Stephen Steiner
To: Erik Newman
Subject: Re: Question

NOVEMBER 9, 2023 / *5:21 PM*

Thank you Erik,

I was getting worried I was blacklisted.

Enjoy your holiday, and please accept my apologies for the emails. I have been suffering in these conditions for two years.

From: Stephen Steiner
To: Rhona S. Kauffman
Subject: Re: Question

NOVEMBER 9, 2023 / *5:43 PM*

I got a call from Erik Newman a few minutes ago. He said he is on vacation and that is why I never heard from him. He also said to call the office and they would email the report to me.

So I called and asked for the report, and the woman said there was not one because they did not find any rat activity during the inspection. And that the entry point he found could be or not be where they are getting in.

They had plenty of time to make up that story.

So I guess I will put back my cams in the crawlspace.

I am about to go insane.

It is deeply concerning that, despite accurately identifying the rodents' point of entry, the exterminator failed to provide a written report—an omission that would have served as critical evidence to hold the HOA accountable for cleanup and repairs. The fact that I was repeatedly unable to reach anyone at the company afterward only heightens my suspicion. Given the significance of the findings, the refusal—or calculated decision—not to furnish documentation raises serious red flags and suggests the possibility of coordinated interference, much like the patterns I experienced with Rhona.

From: Stephen Steiner
  To: Rhona S. Kauffman
Subject: Question

NOVEMBER 9, 2023 / 6:32 PM

I am going to get a home inspection instead of having another exterminator come over and I have to go through the same thing. I want a full inspection of the condo and crawlspace. Then send that report over to the lawyers.

What do you think?

From: Rhona S. Kauffman
  To: Stephen Steiner
Subject: RE: Question

NOVEMBER 9, 2023 / 7:14 PM

Do not tell the inspector that your unit is subject to a potential lawsuit. Just say you want the inspection, or they will not do it.

From: Stephen Steiner
  To: Rhona S. Kauffman
Subject: RE: Question

NOVEMBER 10, 2023 / 1:03 AM

Yep, I will be clueless about everything.

From: Stephen Steiner
  To: Rhona S. Kauffman
Subject: Update

NOVEMBER 11, 2023 / 7:20 AM

Scheduled an appointment with Advantage Inspection Professionals at 8:30 AM on Monday. They use thermal imaging when inspecting.

When I get the report I would like to schedule time to go over and next steps.

From: Advantage Inspection Professionals, LLC
  To: Stephen Steiner
Subject: Inspection

NOVEMBER 11, 2023 / 8:05 AM

Thank you for trusting Advantage Inspection Professionals, LLC to perform the Condominium Inspection on 11/13/2023 at 8:30 AM.

Residential Inspection Fee: $575.00   Total: $575.00

Pre-Payment is required for all inspections and can be done by clicking on this payment link.

Respectfully,
Bruce Carmichael, ASHI, CRT, CMI
Advantage Inspection Professionals, LLC

From: Rhona S. Kauffman
  To: Stephen Steiner
Subject: RE: Update

NOVEMBER 11, 2023 / 9:43 AM

Perfect.

From: Stephen Steiner
  To: Advantage Inspection Professionals, LLC
Subject: RE: Inspection

NOVEMBER 13, 2023 / 2:42 PM

Here is the thermal I took of the ceiling in the condo. Thank you two for coming out
Look forward to getting the report.

A SPECIAL PLACE

From: Bruce Carmichael, ASHI, CRT, CMI
To: Stephen Steiner
Subject: Your Inspection Report

NOVEMBER 13, 2023 / 9:47 PM

See attached electronic PDF copy of the property inspection report and summary completed on 11/13/2023 at 8:30 AM and sent to all authorized parties. It has been a pleasure working with you, and we hope you think of us for your future inspection needs. Recommendations in the report should be addressed prior to the close of escrow to avoid unknown costs associated with any of the call-outs.

Should you have any further questions or need any clarification, please feel free to call.

Thank you for trusting Advantage Inspection Professionals, LLC.

Bruce Carmichael
Advantage Inspection Professionals, LLC

From: Bruce Carmichael, Certified ASHI & CREIA Inspector
To: Stephen Steiner
Subject: Recommended Vendors

NOVEMBER 14, 2023 / 10:30 AM

We thought you might want a list of our recommended vendors. We compiled this list from known contractors that strive to be the best at what they do.

[List of recommended vendors]

Bruce Carmichael
Advantage Inspection Professionals, LLC

From: Stephen Steiner
To: Bruce Carmichael, ASHI, CRT, CMI
Subject: RE: Your Inspection Report

NOVEMBER 14, 2023 / 11:36 AM

Awesome work! I can't wait to see how they get out of this one.

I will keep you posted.

From: Stephen Steiner
To: Bruce Carmichael
Subject: RE: Recommended Vendors

NOVEMBER 14, 2023 / 11:44 AM

Thank you for the list. I will be using them once the HOA repairs all the rat damage.

Appreciate everything you have done!

From: Stephen Steiner
To: Rhona S. Kauffman
Subject: Inspection Report

NOVEMBER 14, 2023 / 11:54 AM

Here it is. From the report, I live in a rat-infested shack.

Let me know if this will work.

A SPECIAL PLACE

Just checking to see if you received the report on Tuesday.

Rhona was fully aware that I would be sending the inspection report on November 14th—evidence that clearly validated my suffering and established the HOA's responsibility for the extensive property damage. Yet, instead of acting with urgency, she waited two full days just to acknowledge receipt. This delay was not accidental. I have every reason to believe she forwarded the report to Shelley and the HOA's legal team during that window, giving them time to strategize a response. Had she been acting in my best interest, her acknowledgment and action would have been immediate. Her inaction speaks volumes.

Yes, I will take a look at it and prepare a response letter to Wayne with the report attached.

Thank you.

After receiving the official inspection report—which unequivocally documented that my condominium was infested with rodents and rendered uninhabitable due to toxic conditions—I immediately forwarded it to Rhona for action. I followed up multiple times, requesting confirmation of receipt. Despite the urgency of the matter, she failed to respond for two full days, finally acknowledging receipt on November 16 at 1:11 PM, more than 48 hours after it was sent. She stated she would prepare a formal response and include the inspection report in a letter to the HOA's legal counsel. That response was never sent.

From November 16 through December 31, I received no updates, no emails, and no communication of any kind from Rhona. She completely ghosted me during a time when critical action was required. Her failure to follow through—especially after receiving such a decisive piece of evidence—was not just negligent; it raises serious ethical concerns and strongly suggests collusion with opposing counsel. Her inaction speaks volumes and constitutes, in my view, a willful breach of her duty to represent my interests.

This email is mostly for documentation. My kitchen lights flicker and have been for a while. I have stopped using them for fear they might start a fire. More than likely, the "ghost rats" have chewed the wires, or they have made a nest on top of one of the light fixtures and the urine is causing the issue.

Have a great Thanksgiving, and I look forward to their response to the inspection report.

The Steiner Report
3155 E Ramon Rd Unit 808
Palm Springs, CA 92264
Monday, November 13, 2023

METHOD OF INSPECTION

Note Viewed the attic area from the attic hatch with a high powered light.

CEILING AND ROOF STRUCTURE TYPE & CONDITION
Stick Framing.

LEAK EVIDENCE
There is no current visible evidence of leakage into the attic area.

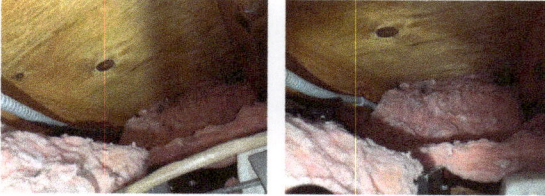

ELECTRICAL

SC All electrical in attic needs to be inspected for damage from rodent activity in attic.

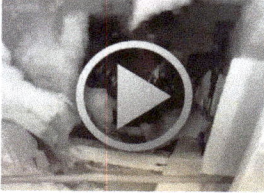

INSULATION TYPE & CONDITION
Fiberglass Batts.

SC Rodent droppings has soiled some of the insulation. Soiled insulation should be removed.

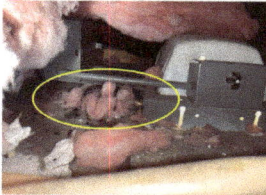

VAPOR RETARDERS
Insulation with attached vapor retarder installed.

The Steiner Report
3155 E Ramon Rd Unit 808
Palm Springs, CA 92264
Monday, November 13, 2023

EXHAUST FAN DUCTING
The bathroom exhaust fans are ducted through the roof.

PESTS
SC I observed evidence of rodents in the attic. Contact HOA for additional information and repair. Contact a Pest Control Operator to further evaluate.

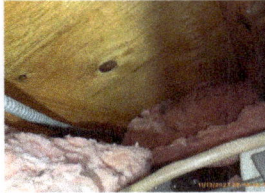

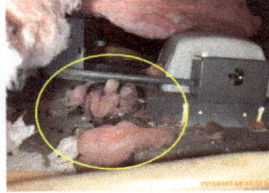

Electrical

An electrical system consist of the service, distribution, wiring and convenience outlets (switches, lights and receptacles). Our examination of the electrical system includes the exposed and accessible conductors, branch circuitry, panels, over current protection devices and a random sampling of convenience outlets. We look of adverse conditions such as improper installation, exposed wiring, running splices, reversed polarity and circuit protection devices. We do not evaluate fusing and/or calculate circuit loads. The hidden nature of the electrical system prevents inspection of every length of wire. Any electrical repairs should be done by a qualified company. The power to the entire house should be turned off prior to beginning any repairs, no matter how trivial the repairs may be. Operation of time clock motors is not verified. Inoperative light fixtures often lack bulbs or have dead bulbs installed. Light bulbs are not changed during the inspection. We make every effort to test all accessible receptacles, switches and fixtures, some may not have been accessible during the inspection and were not tested.

SERVICE UTILITY STATUS
Electric was on

SERVICE
Under ground electrical service laterals are not visible and not inspected.

DISCONNECT TYPE & PANEL RATING
Breakers, Estimated Amperage rating 120/240 volt system, panel rated at 125 Amperes.

MAIN PANEL
Condo/Townhouse disconnect panels are not inspected and not part of this inspection.

MAIN PANEL GROUNDING
Grounding system is present

BONDING
Could not verify

SERVICE WIRING CONDUCTORS
Copper

The Steiner Report
3155 E Ramon Rd Unit 808
Palm Springs, CA 92264
Monday, November 13, 2023

COILS CONDENSATION LINE
Primary condensation line installed.

COILS SECONDARY CONDENSATION LINE

UG Recommend Micro switch be installed on secondary condensation line to prevent moisture damage if primary condensation line becomes blocked.

A/C SECONDARY CONDENSATE DRAIN PAN
NA

RETURN PLENUM
Visible areas of the return plenum was in good condition.

SC Rodent droppings noted inside the return plenum. We recommend further review and repairs by a qualified specialist in the appropriate trade.

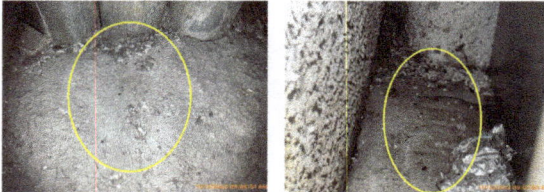

THERMOSTAT CONTROLS
The thermostat was operational at time of inspection

A SPECIAL PLACE

INSPECTION REPORT

Interior Areas

The finished surfaces, hardware, windows and doors of the interior were found to be in generally acceptable condition. Any exceptions are noted in the report. Cosmetic flaws such as stained/worn carpet, marred surface finishes and worn paint that are apparent to the average person are not included in this inspection, although we may not occasionally report them as a courtesy to our clients. Cosmetic flaws such as minor cracks and nail pops occur in all houses. These are typical cosmetic in nature and are caused by settlement and / or shrinkage of building components. Furnishings are not typically moved in the inspection process by the inspector, which limits the inspection to free areas, defects may be blocked from view Blocked or concealed conditions are not the responsibility of the inspector. Determining the souce of odors or like conditions is not a part of this inspection. Floor coverings that are damage or stains may be hidden by furniture. The conditions of underlying floor coverings is not inspected.

OCCUPIED

Note NOTE that if areas of the home are inaccessible or concealed from the inspectors view, then an inspection of that area or item did not take place. Request that any information about any hidden problems be revealed to you about these inaccessible or hidden areas from the seller prior to the close of escrow. Return to the property prior to the close of escrow and perform a walk-through inspection of your own after the owner's belongings have been removed. If your inspection or information reveals hidden damage or concerns contact a qualified specialist or your inspector for a return visit.

WALL AND CEILING TYPE
Textured Drywall

WALLS AND CEILINGS CONDITION

NR Moisture damage noted to ceilings throughout kitchen bedrooms and living room from rodent activity in attic. All ceiling and walls and insulation that had been soiled by rodents needs to be removed. We recommend further review and repairs by a qualified specialist in the appropriate trade.

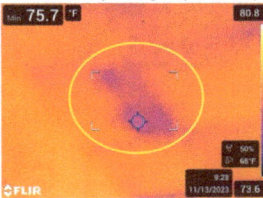

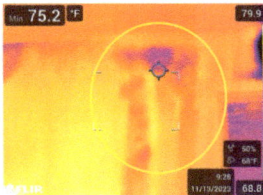

123

The Steiner Report
3155 E Ramon Rd Unit 808
Palm Springs, CA 92264
Monday, November 13, 2023

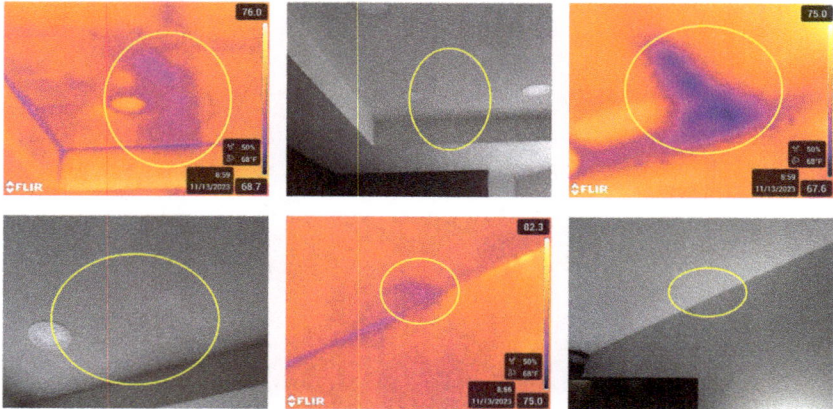

FLOOR CONDITION

Visual examination of unobstructed areas of floor showed no damage at time of inspection. Any small cracks are typical.

THERMAL SCANNING

Note **Advantage Inspection professionals LLC has made a choice to include a limited thermal scan as part of this inspection. There are times when a thermal scan of an area can help the inspector identify a condition that may not be visible without the use of the thermal camera. Thermal photo inclusion is of a localized spot (about 1"x1" square) and in no way meant to give a impression that any other portion of the house/property were viewed with a thermal camera. Only the spot pictured was viewed with the thermal image. This thermal image is used to emphasize or highlight only the condition that was pictured. We always recommend full review of the entire inspection report. A thermal image only detects an anomaly/a surface temperature differential and not anything else and does not see through surfaces or X-ray surfaces. Please visit Flir.com for your due diligence on understanding a thermal photo.**

PHONE-INTERCOM-INTERNET & SECURITY SYSTEMS

NT Phone systems including intercoms, high speed internet, cable,home automation and security systems are not evaluated and not part of this inspection, inquire with seller or owner about condition and usage.

Windows & Doors

Due to wind, dry air, dust and dirt. You will see built up of sand, dust and dirt in your exterior doors and windows and tracks. Regular cleaning is needed for proper operation. Determining the condition of insulated glass windows and doors is not always possible due to temperature, weather and lighting conditions. Dirty windows may make it difficult to determine the exact condition of insulated windows. Check with the seller for further information

MAIN ENTRY DOORS CONDITION

Appeared to be in good working condition at time of inspection, deadbolt is operational.

Mo	Tu	We	Th	Fr	Sa	Su
				~~1~~	~~2~~	~~3~~
~~4~~	~~5~~	~~6~~	~~7~~	~~8~~	~~9~~	10
~~11~~	12	~~13~~	14	~~15~~	~~16~~	17
~~18~~	~~19~~	~~20~~	~~21~~	~~22~~	~~23~~	~~24~~
~~25~~	~~26~~	~~27~~	~~28~~	~~29~~	~~30~~	~~31~~

DECEMBER

536 DAYS
UNRESOLVED

A SPECIAL PLACE

From: Stephen Steiner
To: Rhona S. Kauffman
Subject: Update

DECEMBER 13, 2023 / 7:37 PM

Latest news:

I had a dental appointment last week for a cleaning. My dentist wanted to do X-rays to check because I was grinding due to stress. The X-rays showed the tooth that was causing the pain was cracked and got infected and now has to be pulled.

Any update from them?

This is the physical toll inflicted by Rhona, Shelley, Donna, the HOA Board of Directors, and Seabreeze Management. The relentless episodes of shingles, extreme stress, depression, and the cruelty of being forced to live in a toxic environment directly contributed to a severe medical consequence: I began grinding my teeth so intensely in my sleep that I fractured a molar down the middle. Tragically, this was just one of several serious health issues I would be forced to endure as a direct result of their negligence and inaction.

From: Stephen Steiner
To: Rhona S. Kauffman
Subject: Hello

DECEMBER 19, 2023 / 4:56 PM

I have not heard back from you. I have sent a few emails but no response. I want to sell but cannot until the condo has been cleaned and repaired.

Please let me know where we stand with the HOA.

From: Stephen Steiner
To: Rhona S. Kauffman
Subject: Update

DECEMBER 27, 2023 / 12:41 PM

Is there an update with their lawyers? I need to get this taken care of so I can sell.

Please update me.

From: Stephen Steiner
To: Rhona S. Kauffman
Subject: Happy New Year

DECEMBER 31, 2023 / 12:58 PM

Happy New Year,

Not a happy one for me. I don't know where you went or what happened. I take it from the ghosting that you no longer are representing me.

I wish you all the best in the new year..

From: Rhona S. Kauffman
To: Stephen Steiner
Subject: RE: Happy New Year

DECEMBER 31, 2023 / 1:30 PM

No, I would never ghost you. I've been trying to meet with you in the office and I just found your emails.

Can you meet with me on Thursday?

Just found my emails? How wonderful that you found my emails. How professional of you. Meet with you at the office. No.

2024

Mo	Tu	We	Th	Fr	Sa	Su
1	2	3	4	5	6	7
8	9	10	11	12	13	14
15	16	17	18	19	20	21
22	23	24	25	26	27	28
29	30	31				

JANUARY

567 DAYS
UNRESOLVED

A SPECIAL PLACE

From: Stephen Steiner
To: Rhona S. Kauffman
Subject: RE: Happy New Year

JANUARY 1, 2024 / 9:39PM

I almost gave up hope. A friend told me when he was living in Beverly Hills that he sued his HOA because a rat was living under his porch, and they didn't do anything. He got $50k for pain and suffering. He said that my case was absolutely insane and I should get no less than $10M for all the insanity the HOA and Seabreeze has put me through.

Please please please file the lawsuit. I am going mentally insane from living this way. I don't want to live this way anymore.

I should have terminated the contract then and there. She disappeared for the second half of November and the entirety of December—completely abandoning my case when I needed her most. She protected her former employer instead of me.

From: Stephen Steiner
To: Rhona S. Kauffman
Subject: RE: Happy New Year

JANUARY 2, 2024 / 4:44 PM

I need a time on Thursday. Let me know and I will be there.

From: Rhona S. Kauffman
To: Stephen Steiner
Subject: RE: Happy New Year

JANUARY 2, 2024 / 5:14 PM

Noon—can you meet at noon on Thursday?

From: Stephen Steiner
To: Rhona S. Kauffman
Subject: RE: Happy New Year

JANUARY 3, 2024 / 4:07 AM

I can. See you then.

From: Stephen Steiner
To: Rhona S. Kauffman
Subject: Still working on it

JANUARY 7, 2024 / 7:07 PM

I am trying to get this done, but it is very difficult.

Getting the exact time and day these are taken is not easy since all computers change the date whenever a file is moved or copied.

The video that the inspector used was taken back on Feb 27, 2023.

The fact that a home inspector documented that the entire condo needs to be gutted should be enough. I want them to pay for what they have done to me mentally and physically. I can barely function. The last few days have been extremely bad. The tooth that was cracked became so painful that I had to move the extraction to tomorrow. Send that to the HOA and Seabreeze. Tell them I lost a tooth because of them.

From: Stephen Steiner
To: Rhona S. Kauffman
Subject: ?

JANUARY 8, 2024 / 5:42 PM

Why in November when I sent the inspection report to you did you not send it to the HOA and Seabreeze? I specifically got the report because it was the only option to prove there were rats still accessing it.

And it has been sitting with you for months. That cost me over $600.

It is January now, and not a thing has been done.

I am broke, so I am terminating your service. The only thing you did was send them a demand letter. I am going to sell as is. I don't care anymore. I can't get a response from an email, let alone get a lawsuit going.

From: Rhona S. Kauffman
To: Stephen Steiner
Subject: RE: ?

JANUARY 8, 2024 / 5:56 PM

I did respond to you and asked you to contact the company as they requested but did not hear back from you. However, I am sorry that you feel that way and I will close your file and return the balance of your retainer.

From: Rhona S. Kauffman
To: Stephen Steiner
Subject: Stephan Steiner v. The Palms HOA

JANUARY 8, 2024 / 6:13 PM

Stephen, I just left you a detailed telephone message. Please advise if I can send the below to Wayne, or do you want me to bill you out?

I can send the demand, we can mediate, and then immediately file a lawsuit for their gross negligence. But their defense will be that you need to comply with whatever Phase 2 was with Seabreeze. If Seabreeze fails to move forward, then mediation and a court complaint is necessary.

Please advise either way what you want me to do.

You were my attorney. Had you taken your role seriously and visited my condo even once, you would have understood the severity of the conditions and filed suit the day you were retained. Instead, you chose to play a calculated game—deliberately stalling progress, dragging matters out month after month, and doing the bare minimum necessary to steadily deplete my retainer. Your actions—or lack thereof—were not just negligent; they were strategic, self-serving, and deeply unethical.

From: Rhona S. Kauffman
To: Stephen Steiner
Subject: RE: Still working on it

JANUARY 8, 2024 / 6:14 PM

Also, good luck with the extraction today. I hope it was not too painful.

Thank you, Rhona, for your belated and superficial expression of concern—'hoping it wasn't too painful.' The pain was excruciating. I endured three days of unrelenting agony from a cracked molar—yet another direct consequence of the extreme stress and trauma inflicted by the HOA's negligence and your inaction. Your dismissive response only further highlights your lack of empathy and professional responsibility in handling this matter.

From: Stephen Steiner
To: Scott Fisher
Subject: RE: Responding To Your Recent Contact

JANUARY 9, 2024 / 4:05 PM

The lawyer I hired was a lazy do-nothing. I just had a tooth pulled because of the stress that cracked from grinding.

Is there anything you can do? Call me.

From: Scott Fisher
To: Stephen Steiner
Subject: RE: Responding To Your Recent Contact

JANUARY 9, 2024 / 6:37 PM

Sorry to hear that. Who is your current attorney? Is that attorney based in the desert? Do you know what has been accomplished so far on your behalf?

If you'd rather discuss this by phone, let me know a best range of times to call you tomorrow.

From: Stephen Steiner
To: Scott Fisher
Subject: RE: Responding To Your Recent Contact

JANUARY 10, 2024 / 1:33 PM

Let's talk by phone. She literally did nothing. Let me know a good time when we can talk.

A SPECIAL PLACE

From: Stephen Steiner
To: Rhona S. Kauffman
Subject: Please add to lawsuit

I started a company with my tattoo artist in January of 2023. During this time, I worked from home and dealt with all the rat chaos. It was very difficult but I managed to get product produced and prepared for a show. However, I was sick throughout the year, and when attending the show, I could not focus.

When I returned home, my AC had failed, the unit was 115° and humid, and I was exposed to a stench of urine and feces. The next morning, I developed a skin fungus, which spread quickly.

This entire experience has affected my ability to work. My business partner and I have invested a large amount of money and time, and because of the HOA and Seabreeze, I have lost a lot of income.

My business is at a loss because of them. I had to put everything on hold. This has not only affected me but also my business partner.

From: Stephen Steiner
To: Rhona S. Kauffman
Subject: Design for The Palms

JANUARY 11, 2024 / 5:01 PM

Here are the PDFs for the work I did, which they trashed after I contacted code enforcement.

From: Rhona S. Kauffman
To: Stephen Steiner
Subject: RE: Design for The Palms

JANUARY 11, 2024 / 5:16 PM

Thank you. I am working on everything for you, and I will aggressively pursue on your behalf.

Flat out lie.

From: Stephen Steiner
To: Rhona S. Kauffman
Subject: RE: Design for The Palms

JANUARY 11, 2024 / 6:25 PM

Thank you, Rhona.

From: Rhona S. Kauffman
To: Stephen Steiner
Subject: FW: THE PALMS HOMEOWNERS ASSOCIATION

JANUARY 17, 2024 / 11:00 PM

Good evening, please see the attached response, which I just received in my email as it was in junk mail.

I did send a response, including a demand for mediation and your November inspection report, to Guralnick & Gilliland, LLP as promised. I indicated to them that you did reach out to Seabreeze after receiving the September correspondence, but no one responded, and the HOA never even forwarded you that plan that your neighbor received.

They now allege you did not follow through in contacting Seabreeze. Since this is a potential defense in court, you need to call them tomorrow—contact Mr. Johnson at the number in the attached letter and document who you speak with and what they say. Then email me the details of that communication.

I understand they do not want to repair and replace the entire ceiling and that you have been very sick. I also want you to secure damages from the HOA, so please make sure to call them tomorrow.

"Junk mail"? That excuse is as transparent as it is offensive. For nearly a year, you had no issue receiving my emails—until the one message containing critical evidence that could have advanced or resolved this matter suddenly ends up in your junk folder? Even more troubling is what you said during our phone call after weeks of radio silence: you claimed you never received the inspection report at all. Yet when I forwarded you the very email where you had previously confirmed receipt, you stumbled through an awkward explanation. So which is it? The report never arrived, or it was buried in your junk folder? The timing and inconsistency are far too convenient to be

dismissed as coincidence. I may have been patient and trusting for too long, but I am neither naive nor unaware. This ongoing pattern of evasion, misrepresentation, and inaction raises serious questions about your loyalty and strongly suggests deliberate misconduct and possible collusion with opposing counsel."Yes, Rhona, you sent the demand letter—as I had explicitly told you I did not want to pursue mediation and instead requested that you file a lawsuit. You also eventually submitted the inspection report as promised, but it was two months too late. Had it been sent in a timely manner, it could have been the critical piece of evidence needed to bring an end to my suffering and the ordeal of living in a toxic environment.

In California it is not required to mediate before filing a lawsuit; mediation is considered a voluntary process unless a contract or court order specifically mandates it in a particular case, such as in certain real estate disputes where a mediation clause may be included in the purchase agreement.

Furthermore, shouldn't you have been the one contacting Paul Johnson about Phase 2 and overseeing the cleanup process? As my attorney, it was your responsibility to leverage your legal expertise to compel them to relocate me and ensure that my condo was properly gutted and repaired due to the toxic conditions — conditions that had already made me seriously ill. Instead of advocating for me, you aligned yourself with them.

I was slowly deteriorating, both physically and mentally, yet you still insisted on mediation, despite the fact that I had been living in deplorable, uninhabitable conditions. Meanwhile, the Board and Seabreeze Management deliberately kept all discussions regarding my situation out of the HOA meeting minutes, ensuring there was no official documentation of the hazardous state of my home. I was repeatedly instructed to discuss my concerns with the Seabreeze property manager after the meetings, a clear attempt to avoid transparency and accountability. You were supposed to represent my best interests—yet at every turn, I was left to fight this battle alone.

From: Stephen Steiner
To: Paul Johnson
BCC: Rhona S. Kauffman
Subject: Rodent Clean Up

JANUARY 18, 2024 / 5:26 AM

Please contact me to discuss Phase 2 of the rodent clean and sanitization program.

From: Stephen Steiner
To: Rhona S. Kauffman
Subject: Called and Emailed

JANUARY 18, 2024 / 11:46 AM

I left a message with Paul just now and sent an email earlier today.

From: Rhona S. Kauffman
To: Stephen Steiner
Subject: RE: Called and Emailed

JANUARY 18, 2024 / 11:53 AM

Perfect and thank you.

From: Darren Zetena
To: Stephen Steiner
Subject: The Palms - Steiner, 1355 E Ramon Rd - Unit 808 Attic Rodent Clean-Sanitization

JANUARY 18, 2024 / 5:39 PM

Western Extermination would like to perform Attic Rodent Clean & Sanitization of your unit on Tuesday, January 30, 2024, arriving between 7:00 AM and 9:00 AM. The process will take up to six (6) hours.

Would you please let me know if this date will work for you?

A SPECIAL PLACE

From: Stephen Steiner
To: Darren Zetena
BCC: Rhona S. Kauffman
Subject: RE: The Palms - Steiner, 1355 E Ramon Rd - Unit 808 Attic Rodent Clean-Sanitization

JANUARY 19, 2024 / 7:21 AM

This time works for me, but I have many questions.

The rats have been active in the crawlspace for two years, saturating the insulation with urine and droppings. There is so much in the crawlspace that the ceiling light fixtures are littered with it. The smell in the summer is unbearable when the temperature increases.

How is it possible in six hours to remove all the droppings, rat nests, urine-soaked insulation and drywall, damaged electrical, installation of new insulation and drywall, examination of the air conditioner and heater (rats have accessed it many times), and sanitize the entire ceiling and AC ductwork?

I want to make sure that everyone on the Board, HOA, and Seabreeze Management would feel comfortable and safe living in the condo after the cleanup.

Please give me a call so we can discuss the steps involved in a 6-hour cleanup.

From: Darren Zetena
To: Stephen Steiner
Subject: RE: The Palms - Steiner, 1355 E Ramon Rd - Unit 808 Attic Rodent Clean-Sanitization - Questions

JANUARY 19, 2024 / 12:19 PM

Dear Mr. Steiner,

Thank you for confirming that the date and time work.

I am reviewing your questions and will respond as soon as possible.

In reference to the electrical issue, I have reached out to Horizon Lighting to assess the matter and provide an estimate/proposal. A Horizon Lighting representative will be contacting you to coordinate.

From: Stephen Steiner
To: Rhona S. Kauffman
Subject: RE: Called and Emailed

JANUARY 22, 2024 / 2:16 PM

They are planning on coming out on Jan 30th to do the cleanup. They are only planning on spraying a chemical. I do not want that. They need to gut the condo and do what the inspector documented. I asked Darren to call me to discuss the cleanup.

From: Rhona S. Kauffman
To: Wayne Guralnick
CC: Marilyn Ramos
Subject: FW: The Palms - Steiner, 1355 E Ramon Rd - Unit 808 Attic Rodent Clean-Sanitization

JANUARY 22, 2024 / 7:21 PM

Mr. Guralnick,

Please note that Mr. Steiner has reached out numerous times over the past two years to the HOA and to Seabreeze. He has left multiple messages with Seabreeze management, yet no one ever responded. It was only after my direction that Mr. Steiner emailed Paul Johnson on January 18, 2024, that Darren Zetena finally responded.

Seabreeze has never made any direct effort to verify that the rats were eradicated or check on how this has affected Mr. Steiner. Despite repeated requests, no board members or representatives from Seabreeze have inspected the residence.

Regarding the latest correspondence, Mr. Steiner has not heard any rodent activity in the past four weeks. Please advise on the next steps, as my client has serious concerns about the proposed cleanup.

Thank you, and we look forward to resolving this matter amicably.

GURALNICK & GILLILAND, LLP
ATTORNEYS AT LAW

A FULL SERVICE COMMUNITY
ASSOCIATION LAW FIRM

40-004 COOK STREET, SUITE 3
PALM DESERT, CALIFORNIA 92211
TELEPHONE: (760) 340-1515
FACSIMILE: (760) 568-3053
E-MAIL: WAYNEG@GGHOALAW.COM

PLEASE REFER TO FILE: 84-260

January 22, 2024

SENT VIA EMAIL (Rkauffman@rhonakauffmanlaw.com)
Rhona S. Kauffman, Esq.
Law Offices of Rhona S. Kauffman

Re: Our Client: The Palms Homeowners Association
Your Client: Stephen Steiner, 3155 E. Ramon Road, #808, Palm Springs
("Subject Unit")
Subject: Rodent Infestation

Dear Rhona:

We are baffled as to your email response of January 17, 2024 at 8:44 p.m. alleging that the Association continues to ignore Mr. Steiner. Had it not been for our follow up letter to you on January 10, 2024 (since we had not heard back from you nor had management heard from Mr. Steiner), you would not have sent over the Advantage Inspection Professionals report of November 2023 ("AIP Nov. 2023 Report").

Our original responsive letter to you was dated September 14, 2023. In that letter we stated:

> Phase 2 of Western's proposal (Pages 71 -79 of the enclosed document) could not occur until the Association was assured that there was no further rodent activity at the Subject Unit. Phase 2 is to provide a rodent clean and sanitization program of Your Client's attic (as detailed on page 74).

> We wish to point out that Your Client did not contact the Association after May 2023 about any further rodent activity. In fact, it was the Association's management that was proactive and contacted Mr. Steiner about completing Phase 2 of Western's proposal. Management was then advised by Mr. Steiner that he had legal counsel and ceased further communications.

> The Association has retained Western at a cost of $2,983.00 to perform Phase 2 and just needs Your Client's authorization to facilitate said work at the Subject Unit (but prior to any Phase 2 work, please confirm on behalf of Your Client that he is not aware of any current rodent activity related to his Unit).

Reading this letter from the opposing counsel only reinforces what I've known all along: this entire situation was a coordinated effort to delay, deflect, and protect the HOA from responsibility—at my expense. What stands out most is the claim that they never received the inspection report, despite the fact that Rhona Kauffman confirmed receipt on November 16, 2023, and explicitly stated she would send it along with a response. She never did.

GURALNICK & GILLILAND, LLP.
ATTORNEYS AT LAW

Rhona Kauffman, Esq.
Re: The Palms HOA / Mr. Steiner
Page 2

We don't understand why the AIP Nov. 2023 Report was not provided to us or the Association immediately in November. We also don't understand why the Association was not contacted to report the "alleged" ongoing rodent activity since Western could not proceed with Phase 2 work until all rodent activity had ceased.

You state that Mr. Steiner reached out to management once after our September 2023 letter. Management has no record of any of Your Client's alleged communications between September until last week when management reached out to Your Client.

The Association wants this matter settled as well which prompted our letter of January 10, 2024 since neither management nor our office had heard back from anyone. You claim our email of January 10th ended up in your SPAM folder and that is why you had not responded more timely. We find this difficult to believe since you have received other emails from our office on this matter and other HOA matters with no problem.

Your delay in responding to our September 14, 2023 letter and Mr. Steiner's failure to contact management has been an ongoing issue of lack of communication. At this juncture, the Association needs to know right away if Mr. Steiner is hearing or has seen evidence of rodent activity because they cannot proceed with Western's Phase 2 work until the rodents have been eradicated. You or Your Client need to contact Paul Johnson at paul.johnson@seabreezemgmt.com (and cc: me at WayneG@gghoalaw.com) within 48 hours from the date of this letter. If there is rodent activity, then we need to proceed with the eradication process first before Phase 2 can take place and get the pest control company out there immediately.

We need better and speedier communication from you and Your Client.

Sincerely,

GURALNICK & GILLILAND, LLP

Wayne Guralnick

Wayne Guralnick
/mr

cc: Association

S:\84-260\Letters\Kauffman.ResponseReRodents.012224.wpd

I now believe this was not an oversight, but intentional. This wasn't a case of professional negligence. This was a calculated effort to silence me, discredit me, and allow the HOA to avoid financial liability by dragging out the process until I broke—mentally, physically, and financially.

From: Rhona S. Kauffman
To: Stephen Steiner
Subject: FW: Stephan Steiner v. The Palms HOA

JANUARY 22, 2024 / 5:22 PM

Please see the attached, which we discussed, and my email to the firm on January 17, 2024.

> From: Rhona S. Kauffman
> To: Wayne Guralnick
> Cc: Marilyn Ramos
> Subject: FW: Stephan Steiner v. The Palms HOA
>
> *JANUARY 17, 2024 / 8:42 PM*
>
> Mr. Guralnick,
>
> Attached a report from November 2023 evidencing the ongoing infestation of rodents at my client's residence.
>
> This serious rodent infestation continues to cause my Client significant health issues and on going property damage within his Unit.
>
> He was able to obtain an abatement plan from the Board sent to his neighbor but not to him awhile ago. The Board seems to completely ignore Mr. Steiner's pleas and complaint in regard to this serious manner. Mr. Steiner did reach out to Seabreeze Management following your last correspondence in September but never heard back.
>
> This shall serve as a second demand for the Board to enforce the governing documents and to rectify this horrendous and ongoing problem or in the alternative this shall serve as an immediate demand for Mediation before seeking Court action.
>
> Please confirm receipt. Thank you.
>
> Sincerely,
>
> Rhona S. Kauffman, Esq.
>
> Law Offces of Rhona S. Kauffman

Proof she never sent the inspection report until January 17, 2024.

From: Stephen Steiner
To: Rhona S. Kauffman
Subject: Update

JANUARY 25, 2024 / 10:26 PM

A couple of days ago, my right eye started to become irritated and burn. It worsened in the evening, so I went to bed. When I woke up, the right side of my face was paralyzed. I thought it was due to the extraction, but that was on the left side of my face. I went to my dentist this morning, and he said the gums healed nicely, but it could possibly be Bell's Palsy. The stress from this condo has now caused half my face to be paralyzed.

I received a text from Western Exterminators that they will be coming out on the 29th to cut access points to clean and sanitize the space. I will film all of it. This is going to be very bad.

I am going to make an appointment with my doctor. Thanks to the HOA and Seabreeze, I now have a paralyzed face.

Yes, the unrelenting stress I endured—stemming directly from your failure to represent me—led to a severe shingles outbreak that ultimately caused Bell's Palsy. While you stood by and allowed Shelley, Donna, the HOA Board, the exterminators, and Seabreeze Management to delay, deflect, and deny responsibility, my health deteriorated to the point where I lost function on one side of my face and began to lose vision in my right eye. Your collective inaction and indifference weren't just negligent—they were inhumane. You enabled and prolonged my suffering while disregarding your professional duty and basic human decency.

From: Rhona S. Kauffman
To: Stephen Steiner
Subject: RE: Update

JANUARY 25, 2024 / 12:43 PM

That's terrible. Please keep me updated on your health, of course, because that comes first.

Thanks for your concern. Another lie.

A SPECIAL PLACE

From: Stephen Steiner
To: Rhona S. Kauffman
Subject: RE: Update

JANUARY 29, 2024 / 9:00 AM

CALL MEEEE!

This was an incredibly distressing day for me. Because I reluctantly agreed to proceed with Phase 2 of the so-called Rodent Exclusion Plan—largely due to Rhona's incompetence—two exterminators were sent to my condo to create yet another opening in the ceiling and set additional traps.

The moment they arrived, I became overwhelmed with anxiety. It was immediately clear that this was yet another manufactured delay, this time under the guise of needing to enlarge the existing access panel in the laundry area. None of it made logical or technical sense. I attempted to call Rhona for immediate guidance, but she failed to answer. I followed up with a text message, and when she finally returned my call, I insisted she come to my home to witness firsthand what was being done.

Predictably, she deflected and changed the subject. It was exactly the kind of evasive behavior I had come to expect from her. Realizing I was once again being manipulated and left unprotected, I told the exterminators to leave my property. This entire ordeal was being orchestrated deliberately—and I refused to be complicit in another round of calculated stalling and psychological torment.

From: Rhona S. Kauffman
To: Stephen Steiner
Subject: RE: Update

JANUARY 29, 2024 / 11:09 AM

I'm so sorry to hear about your eye. I will call you later this afternoon after meetings.

From: Stephen Steiner
To: Rhona S. Kauffman
Subject: RE: Update

JANUARY 29, 2024 / 11:11 AM

Sorry, had a freak out moment. Call me back please.

From: Darren Zetena
To: Stephen Steiner
CC: Paul Johnson
Subject: RE: The Palms - Steiner, 1355 E Ramon Rd - Unit 808 Attic Rodent Clean-Sanitization - Tuesday 01-30-2024

JANUARY 29, 2024 / 1:45 PM

Dear Mr. Steiner,

I just received confirmation from Western Extermination that they will be at your home tomorrow, Tuesday, 01-30-2024, between 8:00 AM and 9:00 AM to perform the rodent clean-up work.

Please reply to confirm receipt of this communication.

From: Stephen Steiner
To: Rhona S. Kauffman
Subject: RE: Update

JANUARY 29, 2024 / 4:42 PM

Here is the short of what happened today.

Two guys came this morning to make the holes. When they were talking about making the laundry room hole bigger I began to panic. I didn't want to live through more holes and more dust and smell and getting sick again. I spoke to them in a loud stern voice and asked why I as a human and being forced to live in this environment when anyone of the HOA, Seabreeze,or any of the lawyers would never live in this condo. I reminded them how sick and exhausted I am of Seabreeze playing a game with my life and treating me like this am nothing. They understood and told me Western Exterminators is under new management. The left and said they will discuss with Seabreeze.

About an hour and a half later the two returned and two additional exterminators came over. They went through the condo and discussed where it would be possible to do the sanitization spray. They realized that with the shots of my video and accessing the crawlspace that there is limited room and would be very difficult to clean up all the droppings and insulation. I explained that I did not want any of the urine soaked insulation and droppings in the crawlspace because even though they claimed the spray neutralizes and kills all the bacteria it is still there and I like any homeowner does not want that above their heads. They agreed and said they will still use the fog spray but in the end it needs to all be removed.

They said they will write up a report that the ceiling and walls and everything needs to be removed and replaced and that living in this is toxic.

So we will see what transpires.

I still want to sue for mental, emotional and physical damage they did to me. I do not want to let the get away with this. They ruined my life because they wanted too. They were completely aware of what they were doing. It was a game they played with my life and I want them to compensate me for all the suffering.

I went to the ER yesterday and I have Bells Palsy. They put me on steroids to help. It was caused by my shingles which is a direct result from the massive stress caused by the HOA and Seabreeze. I lost my tooth because of grinding my teeth in my sleep due to the same thing.

Explain to them that they were slowly poisoning me and did nothing but increase the dose because they could. Instead of helping me they poisoned me and didn't give it a care in the world. Never a second thought or let alone a thought of my wellbeing. Maybe a call or email to see how I was doing? Nothing. Absolutely Nothing.

If their lawyers come back with another stupid assume remark please file a lawsuit in a dollar amount you feel appropriate if one of your family members were put through what I went through.

From: Stephen Steiner
To: Rhona S. Kauffman
Subject: Update Jan 30

JANUARY 30, 2024 / 5:57 PM

I hope this message finds you well. I wanted to update you on the recent developments regarding the cleaning process in my unit.

This morning, two cleaning men inspected the cleanup areas (closet and laundry). They concluded that a comprehensive cleaning is only achievable if the unit undergoes a complete gutting. During vacuuming, they discovered and removed a decaying rat above the laundry area.

Seabreeze has no alternative but to proceed with gutting my unit. However, I anticipate they might attempt to prolong the process.

When the cleanup commences, I plan to document everything. This will serve as evidence of the health and property damage I have endured.

The exterminators will be reporting back to Seabreeze with their recommendation: gutting the condo. They also identified openings in the closet of the air conditioner/heater unit that require sealing. They proposed a comprehensive check on all electrical systems, replacement of insulation, and closure of any openings.

I am concerned Seabreeze may attempt to delay the resolution. Please advise on the best course of action for our next steps.

A SPECIAL PLACE

From: donotreply@cincsystems.net   *FEBRUARY 2, 2024 / 12:06 PM*
  To: Stephen Steiner
Subject: The Palms - New Community Association Manager - Darren Zetena

Dear The Palms Homeowners,

I am pleased to announce that I will be your new Community Association Manager. I will be your point person for all matters involving The Palms.

Should an issue arise, or a matter needs to be addressed on the property, please reach out to me via the web portal, email, or telephone.

Sincerely,
Darren Zetena
Senior Community Association Manager

From: Rhona S. Kauffman   *FEBRUARY 5, 2024 / 2:54 PM*
  To: Stephen Steiner
Subject: RE: Update Jan 30

OK, SEND ME THEIR REPORT AND DID THEY NOTIFY THE HOA OF THEIR INVESTIGATION RESULTS? I ALSO WANT TO CONFIRM THEY WILL PAY FOR YOU TO RELOCATE DURING GUTTING. WHAT DO YOU HAVE IN WRITING FROM WESTERN IN THIS REGARD?

Rhona, your email is absolutely infuriating and further proof that you were never truly on my side. I hired you to handle this nightmare—not to sit back and ask me for reports, confirmations, and paperwork while I was battling constant illness, extreme stress, and ultimately developed Bell's palsy from the sheer physical toll of what your inaction and the HOA's cruelty put me through.

You dare ask me to send you Western's report? That's your job. You're the attorney. You should have demanded every single document, followed up with the HOA and Western directly, and ensured—without me lifting another finger—that relocation, remediation, and full accountability were pursued aggressively. But you didn't. You never have. Instead, you repeatedly delayed, deflected, and left me to fight this battle alone while you played both sides.

Your question about what I have in writing from Western is disgusting. You know damn well I've been blacklisted, ghosted, and lied to by vendors—just like I was by you. You know this is HOA property. You know I was forced to live in filth and rot, breathing contaminated air in a condo that multiple exterminators confirmed was unsafe. And now, you're playing the "what do you have in writing" card to cover your own failure to act? Absolutely shameful.

Western Exterminator cleaned up a small section of the crawlspace. A very small section. That's not a solution—that's an insult. The entire crawlspace was contaminated. You've seen the images and videos I documented. You saw the inspection report that said the unit had to be gutted. But instead of fighting for me, you delayed so long and did so little that I ended up with nerve damage and partial facial paralysis. Bell's palsy. From stress. From you. From them. From all of it.

Let's be clear: you were supposed to protect me. You did the opposite. You helped them bury me.

2   ⓘ   (See p. 76)

A SPECIAL PLACE

From: Rhona S. Kauffman
To: Stephen Steiner
Subject: FW: Stephen Steiner - THE PALMS HOMEOWNERS ASSOCIATION

Please see my email below sent to attorneys.

> From: Rhona S. Kauffman
> To: Wayne Guralnick
> Cc: Marilyn Ramos
> Subject: Stephen Steiner - THE PALMS HOMEOWNERS ASSOCIATION
>
> *FEBRUARY 5, 2024, 1:07 PM*
>
> Dear Mr. Guralnik,
>
> We wanted to update you on the investigation into the cleanup and property damage from the rat infestation in Mr. Steiner's residence.
>
> On January 30, 2024, Seabreeze sent the exterminators from Western to the residence to evaluate the infestation and damage to the property. Two cleaning men inspected the cleanup areas (specifically the closet and laundry), and their assessment concluded that a comprehensive cleaning is only achievable if the unit undergoes a complete gutting. They proceeded to vacuum the specified areas and, during the process, discovered and removed a decaying rat situated above the laundry area. Additionally, they identified openings in the closet of the air conditioner/heater unit that require sealing. They proposed a comprehensive check on all electrical systems, replacement of insulation, and closure of any openings.
>
> By now, Seabreeze has received a full report to confirm the above. The HOA has no alternative but to proceed with gutting the unit and the other recommendations from their own exterminator. Please advise as to how soon can we expect this process of a complete gutting of the residence? Mr. Steiner continues to suffer from serious health related issues due to the contamination of his Unit. Also will the HOA agree to temporarily relocate Mr. Steiner during this gutting process?
>
> Thank you.
>
> Sincerely,
> Rhona S. Kauffman, Esq.
> Law Offices of Rhona S. Kauffman

This email is a perfect example of Rhona S. Kauffman's complete failure to act with urgency, conviction, or competence as my legal representative. After nearly a year of delays, repeated pleas, medical deterioration—including Bell's palsy, ongoing shingles outbreaks, and psychological trauma—this is the best she could muster? A soft, lukewarm, bureaucratic note filled with vague phrasing and passive observations that essentially excuses the HOA while pretending to be advocating for me?

Where is the demand for immediate action? Where is the legal pressure? Where is the accountability? She admits in this email that Western Exterminators confirmed the presence of a decaying rat, needed electrical evaluations, missing insulation, and the requirement to gut the unit. And yet, she still phrases her email like a polite request for guidance instead of the urgent legal demand it should have been.

Let's be very clear: this is HOA property that was allowed to fester into a health hazard. It was their contractors, their vendors, their delays, and Rhona's own negligence that forced me to live in a rodent-infested hellhole for over a year. And what does Rhona do? She asks, "Please advise how soon we can expect the gutting process to begin" — as if we're discussing a casual remodel, not the aftermath of a completely preventable and life-altering disaster.

This wasn't advocacy. This was theater—a performative gesture to cover up her role in dragging this out, draining my health, my finances, and my will to keep going. She did this to protect her former employer, to appease the HOA, and to gaslight me while pretending to represent my interests. She knew exactly what she was doing. This email proves it.

She should have demanded immediate relocation, threatened legal action, and sent this letter months earlier—right after the inspection report in November. Instead, she ghosted me for six weeks, then returned with this pathetic excuse for representation. Enough is enough.

From: Stephen Steiner
To: Rhona S. Kauffman
Subject: RE: Update Jan 30

I have nothing in writing, but I will contact Chad and get one.

Two exterminators came to the condo in the morning to make holes to prep for the cleaning the next day. When they opened the original access points (laundry and bedroom), they realized there was not enough room to clean. They left to discuss with their boss and later returned with two additional exterminators.

They concluded that the entire condo needs to be gutted and that they will send a report to Seabreeze.

I sent a text to Chad requesting the report.

From: Stephen Steiner
To: Rhona S. Kauffman
Subject: Re: FW: Stephen Steiner - THE PALMS HOMEOWNERS ASSOCIATION

FEBRUARY 6, 2024 / 8:58 AM

Email is perfect.

From: Stephen Steiner
To: Rhona S. Kauffman
Subject: Re: FW: Stephen Steiner - THE PALMS HOMEOWNERS ASSOCIATION

FEBRUARY 9, 2024 / 4:48 PM

No response from Western about getting the report or if they spoke to Seabreeze.

Face still paralyzed.

From: Stephen Steiner
To: Rhona S. Kauffman
Subject: Finally heard back

FEBRUARY 12, 2024 / 2:56 PM

This is the text from Chad at Western:

> *Good morning Steve. Sorry for the long delay but I have not heard anything from Seabreeze if they want to move forward with the work.*

Either they are pricing out what needs to be done, or they are delaying once again.

From: Rhona S. Kauffman
To: Stephen Steiner
Subject: FW: Stephen Steiner - THE PALMS HOMEOWNERS ASSOCIATION

FEBRUARY 12, 2024 / 4:29 PM

Please see my email of today sent.

> From: Rhona S. Kauffman
> To: Wayne Guralnick
> Cc: Marilyn Ramos
> Importance: High
> Subject: RE: Stephen Steiner - THE PALMS HOMEOWNERS ASSOCIATION
>
> *FEBRUARY 12, 2024 / 2:29 PM*
>
> Good afternoon,
>
> We sent the below status email to you on February 5, 2024.
>
> Mr. Steiner has not heard back from the HOA but received this text this morning form Chad at Western Exterminators.
>
> > *Good morning Steve. Sorry for the long delay but I have not heard anything from Seabreeze if they want to move forward with the work.*
>
> Please advise as to the status of this work that needs to be completed asap.
>
> Thank you
>
> Sincerely,
> Rhona S. Kauffman, Esq.
> Law Offices of Rhona S. Kauffman

From: Stephen Steiner
To: Rhona S. Kauffman
Subject: Re: FW: Stephen Steiner - THE PALMS HOMEOWNERS ASSOCIATION

FEBRUARY 12, 2024 / 4:36 PM

Thanks, Rhona.

If they continue to drag this out, do we file a lawsuit?

From: Stephen Steiner
To: Rhona S. Kauffman
Subject: Access

FEBRUARY 12, 2024 / 10:05 PM

The access point that the exterminators made failed and fell from the ceiling. I don't know how long it has been open, but I am sure it fell along with the rat into my closet.

Thank the HOA and Seabreeze for making my life so horrible.

From: Giuseppe Vezzoli
To: Stephen Steiner
Subject: Fwd: The Palms - 02-24-2024 Board Meeting Agenda

FEBRUARY 16, 2024 / 4:55 PM

Did you get this?

From: Stephen Steiner
To: Giuseppe Vezzoli
Subject: Re: The Palms - 02-24-2024 Board Meeting Agenda

FEBRUARY 16, 2024 / 5:41 PM

Yep, just got it. Thanks for checking. I want to be there to show Shelley, the board, and Seabreeze that their actions made half my face paralyzed.

From: Stephen Steiner
To: Rhona S. Kauffman
Subject: February HOA Meeting

FEBRUARY 16, 2024 / 7:49 PM

I have attached the HOA February Meeting agenda, and I noticed they failed to include my rat problem in the list of unfinished business.

They are purposely doing nothing. Can you give them a deadline and, if they do not start the process, file a lawsuit?

Why is nothing happening? Is my life that worthless to everyone? None of them would live in the conditions I am living in.

Are they waiting for me to do something that will justify putting a lien on my property? What is wrong with them? Do they think what they are doing is right?

From: Stephen Steiner
To: Darren Zetena
Subject: The Palms - Steiner, 1355 E Ramon Rd - Unit 808 - Rodent

FEBRUARY 26, 2024 / 9:38 AM

I have attached videos of the rodents and sending the thermal video separately (file too large to attach to this email). On the thermal footage all the black spots are areas where they have urinated and pooped or have nested. In my second bedroom there is so much urine that it is coming down the wall. This is throughout my entire condo. I have checked with neighbors (Unit 810) and they have none. I stopped filming last summer when the rats chewed the power cable to the camera. So the amount or excrement has probably doubled.

On a side note, I have not used my dishwasher or lights in the kitchen for over a year. The smell when the dishwasher is running is unbearable. It is a new dishwasher that I purchased when we were remodeling. It is linked to the pipe that the rats have chewed to gain access to my unit. The lights flicker now and I fear the rats have damaged the wiring and will start a fire. The lights are also new. I took a snapshot of a rat chewing on a wire.

From: Darren Zetena
To: Stephen Steiner
Subject: The Palms - Steiner, 1355 E Ramon Rd - Unit 808 - Rodent

FEBRUARY 26, 2024 / 10:20 AM

Could you please call me as soon as possible so that I can get additional information on the rodent issue that you mentioned at the **02-24-2024** Board Meeting during Open Forum at the end of the meeting?

From: Stephen Steiner
To: Darren Zetena
Subject: Re: The Palms - Steiner, 1355 E Ramon Rd - Unit 808 - Rodent

FEBRUARY 26, 2024 / 11:38 AM

I have attached videos of the rodents and will send the thermal video separately (file too large to attach to this email). On the thermal footage, all the black spots are areas where they have urinated, pooped, or nested. In my second bedroom, there is so much urine that it is coming down the wall. This is throughout my entire condo. I have checked with neighbors (Unit 810), and they have none. I stopped filming last summer when the rats chewed the power cable to the camera, so the amount of excrement has probably doubled.

On a side note, I have not used my dishwasher or lights in the kitchen for over a year. The smell when the dishwasher is running is unbearable. It is a new dishwasher I purchased when we were remodeling, and it is linked to the pipe the rats have chewed to gain access to my unit. The lights flicker now, and I fear the rats have damaged the wiring and will start a fire. The lights are also new. I took a snapshot of a rat chewing on a wire.

Thanks for getting back to me so quickly.

From: Stephen Steiner
To: Darren Zetena
Subject: Thermal Video

FEBRUARY 26, 2024 / 11:39 AM

(Attachment sent separately)

From: Darren Zetena
To: Stephen Steiner
Subject: RE: The Palms - Steiner, Unit #808 - Thermal Video

FEBRUARY 26, 2024 / 1:44 PM

Dear Mr. Steiner,

This is to confirm receipt. Thank you.

From: Stephen Steiner
To: Darren Zetena
Subject: Re: The Palms - Steiner, Unit #808 - Thermal Video

FEBRUARY 26, 2024 / 1:45 PM

Thank you, Darren.

Mo	Tu	We	Th	Fr	Sa	Su
				~~1~~	~~2~~	~~3~~
~~4~~	~~5~~	~~6~~	~~7~~	~~8~~	~~9~~	10
~~11~~	12	13	14	15	16	17
18	19	20	21	22	23	24
25	26	27	28	29	30	~~31~~

MARCH

627 DAYS
UNRESOLVED

From: Stephen Steiner
   To: Rhona S. Kauffman
Subject: Update

MARCH 1, 2024 / 2:58 AM

Have their lawyers or Seabreeze come to a decision? It has been over two weeks.

From: Rhona S. Kauffman
   To: Stephen Steiner
Subject: Response

MARCH 1, 2024 / 9:49 AM

Please advise this was received today. We can discuss this as soon as you're available today or Monday.

From: Stephen Steiner
   To: Rhona S. Kauffman
Subject: Re: Response

MARCH 1, 2024 / 1:37 PM

I left a message. Please call me

From: Stephen Steiner
   To: Rhona S. Kauffman
Subject: Re: Response

MARCH 1, 2024 / 1:57 PM

I am done. It is all pointless. It will drag out forever. I will never win this battle. I am completely broke and sick. My life is a series of disappointments. I am going to put it up for sale and move.

Thank you for your work. I am ending the contract. I cannot afford this anymore.

From: Stephen Steiner
   To: Rhona S. Kauffman
Subject: Re: Response

MARCH 1, 2024 / 1:58 PM

Please let them know that they have to come repair the three holes they made in my ceiling.

From: Stephen Steiner
   To: Rhona S. Kauffman
Subject: Re: Response

MARCH 1, 2024 / 2:00 PM

I will let them know to repair the ceiling. It will cost me for you to do that. Sorry.

From: Stephen Steiner
   To: Rhona S. Kauffman
Subject: Email Chain

MARCH 4, 2024 / 4:27 PM

Once again, I apologize for my behavior. I don't handle stress well anymore. I can barely see out of my right eye and I have a bad case of shingles.

I have attached the chain of emails with dates and times in red.

On a side note, they have no right to comment on the cleanliness of my condo since none of them have ever set foot inside.

Can you please let them understand that regardless of everything, it is the HOA's responsibility to clean the crawlspace? I have been patient for two years, three extermination companies, and a slew of exterminators making holes, setting traps, and accomplishing nothing.

I think they do not understand that this is not an issue that can be considered "closed." Their approach is ridiculous. If they close it, I place a ticket on the portal about a rat in my crawlspace. There, it's open again.

From: Stephen Steiner
To: Rhona S. Kauffman
Subject: Question

MARCH 6, 2024 / 5:59 PM

So what is next? I am not going to be able to last much longer in this condo. It is making me horribly sick. I cannot take another attack of shingles and possibly going blind.

If they plan on dragging this out, I am going to sell. To them, it's a game. They have no idea the suffering they have put me through. The Board and Seabreeze destroyed my life. I have nothing left.

From: Stephen Steiner
To: Rhona S. Kauffman
Subject: My response to their letter - Please confirm receipt

MARCH 14, 2024 / 5:48 AM

Please inform Seabreeze and the HOA's lawyers that I explicitly requested, as documented in my emails to Donna, that the access points not be installed in my ceiling but rather on the roof.

Despite this, they insisted on placement in my unit, resulting in the documented damage and toxic waste from rats. Donna assured me that Seabreeze would address the cleanup and repair the holes, emphasizing that according to the CCRs, the HOA is responsible for everything above the ceiling.

From: Rhona S. Kauffman
To: Stephen Steiner
Subject: Re: My response to their letter - Please confirm receipt

MARCH 14, 2024 / 8:33 AM

Let's set up a telephone call to discuss everything. When are you available tomorrow?

From: Stephen Steiner
To: Rhona S. Kauffman
Subject: Re: My response to their letter - Please confirm receipt

MARCH 14, 2024 / 11:39 AM

11 AM works for me.

From: Rhona S. Kauffman
To: Stephen Steiner
Subject: RE: My response to their letter - Please confirm receipt

MARCH 14, 2024 / 11:41 AM

You got it—talk tomorrow.

From: Stephen Steiner
To: Rhona S. Kauffman
Subject: RE: My response to their letter - Please confirm receipt

MARCH 14, 2024 / 11:43 AM

Great!

GURALNICK & GILLILAND, LLP
ATTORNEYS AT LAW

A FULL SERVICE COMMUNITY
ASSOCIATION LAW FIRM

40-004 COOK STREET, SUITE 3
PALM DESERT, CALIFORNIA 92211
TELEPHONE: (760) 340-1515
FACSIMILE: (760) 568-3053
E-MAIL: WAYNEG@GGHOALAW.COM

PLEASE REFER TO FILE: 84-260

March 1, 2024

SENT VIA EMAIL (Rkauffman@rhonakauffmanlaw.com)
Rhona S. Kauffman, Esq.
Law Offices of Rhona S. Kauffman

Re: **Our Client:**   **The Palms Homeowners Association**
     Your Client: **Stephen Steiner, 3155 E. Ramon Road, #808,**
                       Palm Springs ("Subject Unit")
     Subject: **Rodent Infestation**

Dear Rhona:

We have communicated with the Association regarding the Subject Unit and the additional remediation work Mr. Steiner has requested. We wish to point out that as it pertains to maintenance, the CC&Rs provide:

    3.   _Maintenance_. **Each owner of a condominium shall be responsible for maintaining his unit, including the equipment and fixtures in the unit, and its interior walls, ceilings, windows and doors in a clean, sanitary, workable and attractive condition,** _and shall maintain in an open and unobstructed condition all sewer and drainage pipes and lines serving his own unit between the points at which the same enter said unit and the points at which same join sewer and drainage pipes and lines serving other units. ... Unless otherwise provided in this declaration, each owner shall clean and maintain any exclusive easement appurtenant to his condominium._ (emphasis added)

As to the duties of the Association:

    (1)   _Operation and Maintenance of Common Area and Recreation Area_. _To operate, maintain, and otherwise manage or provide for the operation, maintenance and management of the common area and the recreation area, and all its facilities, improvements, and landscaping including any private driveways and private streets, and any other property acquired by the Association, including personal property, in a first- class condition and in a good state of repair. ..._

GURALNICK & GILLILAND, LLP.
ATTORNEYS AT LAW

Rhona Kauffman, Esq.
Re: The Palms HOA / Mr. Steiner
Page 2

It is clear that Owners are responsible for the interior of their Units (including keeping the Unit in sanitary condition) and the Association is responsible for the common areas. The Association has followed the advice of its pest control consultant related to rodent control in the common areas including mitigating access points with the assistance of professionals / third party vendors. Despite your frivolous claims, the Association did not breach its standard of care in regards to rodent control.

Conversely, the ongoing matter at the Steiner unit has been frustrated and made worse by delays and inaction by Mr. Steiner and/or his counsel (as has been addressed in our prior communications and incorporated herein by this reference). Mr. Steiner has not been cooperative with the Association and weeks at a time would go by before he would respond to the Association (or before you would respond to our correspondence). These delays by you and your client are not the fault of the Association.

We understand that Western completed Phase 2 of their proposal on January 30, 2024, which the Association generously paid for as promised. However, we emphasize that the Association is NOT responsible for any work inside the interior of the Unit. Any further work to the Unit will be up to Mr. Steiner to handle, negotiate and pay for. His failure to mitigate any supposed damage to the interior of this Unit is not the Association's issue.

We wish to note that at the Board's February 24, 2024 meeting, Mr. Steiner suggested he may have had another rodent but also stated that he would not allow anyone into his Unit to treat for said rodent. This was stated in a public forum and heard by several witnesses.

Despite his representation at the February 24th meeting, Mr. Steiner did allow the Association's pest control to enter the Unit; however, he would not allow them to set any traps (see enclosed email). In light of all of the foregoing, the Association will not be taking any further action regarding your client's Unit.

Sincerely,

GURALNICK & GILLILAND, LLP

Wayne Guralnick

Wayne Guralnick
/mr

Encl.
cc: Association

S:\84-260\Letters\Kauffman.Final.030124.wpd

This letter is outrageous and full of falsehoods. First of all, the claim that my unit was unsanitary is complete nonsense. I have OCD and was constantly cleaning because of the rats — the infestation wasn't in my living space, it was in the crawlspace, which is HOA property. None of these people ever stepped foot in my home, so how would they even know?

From: Rhona S. Kauffman
To: Stephen Steiner
Subject: Telephone Conference

Thank you for speaking with me today. I understand your frustration with the HOA's failure to act.

We discussed that you MUST allow the pest control companies and/or the contractors sent by the HOA to do their work—whatever that may be—or they will continue to hold it against you as they have in the past. You told me they wanted to cut another hole and you said no (which I understand), but you have two choices:

1. Let them proceed.
2. Hire an expert.

Since you want to sell your unit, you need clearance on the rats before listing it. I recommend disclosure unless the pest control company confirms the rats are 100% eradicated. If you cannot afford an expert (e.g., an engineer or architect) to determine the source of the intrusion, you must allow those sent by the HOA to investigate.

Let me know next week how things are going. Have a nice weekend.

Your email is yet another clear example of your complete failure to advocate for your client—and further evidence that you are actively aligned with the opposing counsel's interests. Your suggestion that I must either allow the HOA's contractors to proceed without question, or personally pay to hire an expert to do their job for them, is both legally inaccurate and professionally irresponsible.

Let me remind you, for what should be the hundredth time: the crawlspace and all structures above the ceiling are the legal responsibility of the HOA, as defined by the governing documents of the community and California common interest development law. I am not required to pay out-of-pocket to investigate, treat, or repair infestations occurring in HOA-maintained property. Your failure to assert this fundamental point on my behalf is not just negligent—it is willful malpractice.

Your suggestion that I must cooperate with an endless series of disruptive, ineffective "inspections" or else be blamed for delays is outrageous. I have endured over two years of physical and psychological torment, including Bell's palsy, chronic shingles outbreaks, and severe emotional trauma because of your refusal to hold the HOA accountable. Your position—that my only choices are to allow further intrusion or spend thousands of dollars on experts—is completely unacceptable and shows blatant disregard for my legal rights and wellbeing.

You were retained to protect me. Instead, you've allowed the HOA and Seabreeze to prolong and intensify my suffering, and now you have the audacity to send a dismissive "Have a nice weekend" after more than twelve months of systemic neglect and abuse.

Let the record show: Your ongoing mishandling of this matter, including misrepresenting legal obligations, refusing to file appropriate claims or lawsuits, and repeatedly deflecting blame onto me—your client—is definitive evidence of a conflict of interest and dereliction of duty.

From: Stephen Steiner
To: Rhona S. Kauffman
Subject: Re: Telephone Conference

I feel deeply frustrated because I followed through on all your requests diligently. I even arranged a home inspection, yet the necessary documents weren't forwarded immediately, leading to this outcome.

It baffles me why people disregard past actions. They had no genuine interest in resolving the issue. Donna's relocation to another property is undeniable evidence. They prolonged the problem, knowing it would wear me down.

I enlisted your services to put an end to their manipulative tactics. If this had happened to a board member or another homeowner, swift action would have been taken. Instead, I have consistently faced mistreatment.

Ultimately, I find myself shouldering the blame once again, bringing this painful chapter to another disheartening conclusion.

A SPECIAL PLACE

From: Rhona S. Kauffman
To: Stephen Steiner
Subject: Re: Telephone Conference

You are not to blame. We just need to work toward resolving your rat problem and move forward for your benefit.

That's correct—I am not at fault. You are responsible, due to your gross incompetence and your repeated failure to represent me with the diligence and duty required of legal counsel.

From: Rhona S. Kauffman
To: Stephen Steiner
Subject: Re: Telephone Conference

The issue stems from September when you were required to reach out to Western. You told me you sent them messages, but they claim they never received them. The report you provided in November was forwarded in December, which was a minor issue compared to what they're now alleging—that you delayed reaching out between September and December.

When you left my office in September, you promised to contact them, but I have several emails where I asked if you had done so, and you didn't confirm. Unfortunately, they will use this against you, arguing that you delayed getting Western involved.

The most recent issue is that you did not allow the contractor to make a new hole in your ceiling. While I understand your reasoning, the problem is that you cannot afford to hire experts to fix this yourself. Therefore, you need to accept help from those willing to assist for free. That way, you can list the property for sale as we discussed.

Alternatively, we can still pursue the HOA through mediation to demand a complete cleanup of your unit. However, this would require a replenishing retainer. The HOA might refuse mediation, claiming you delayed allowing Western access. I would argue that they failed to respond in a timely manner.

I want you to understand that I'm not saying you don't have a case. However, in civil litigation, a legal defense called "Laches" may apply. Laches means that if a plaintiff delays taking action to the extent that it harms the defendant, they may be barred from pursuing legal action. The HOA could argue that your delay in September prevents further claims. However, since the rodent issue is ongoing, I believe this argument is irrelevant.

If you want me to insist on mediation, I will write to Wayne and demand it again, but I need a replenishing retainer. Additionally, we need confirmation that the HOA's vendor attempted repairs first. Please let me know how you'd like to proceed.

Reading Rhona's response is infuriating—an astonishing display of deflection, negligence, and outright manipulation. From the very beginning, I hired her to represent me, not to blame me for the inaction and delays that were entirely her responsibility. Her job was to contact Western Exterminators and push the HOA for accountability. Instead, she sat back, let deadlines pass, and now has the audacity to claim that I somehow caused the delays? Absolutely not.

Her claim that I "promised" to contact Western is a complete fabrication. I never assumed that role. The last official contact I had was when Nick Valek passed the torch to Chad McChesney, who showed up once and never returned. From that point forward, no one came, no traps were checked, and I was left to live with the stench, maggots, flies, and psychological torment—alone.

Her tone in this email reveals everything: dismissive, condescending, and devoid of urgency. Her proposal to "cut a new hole" as if that's a rational solution after everything I've endured is not only tone-deaf—it's abusive. And let's not forget: everything above my ceiling is HOA property. Why should I pay for experts or suffer further damage to my home when the law is clear?

This isn't advocacy—it's sabotage dressed in legalese.

And despite my worsening health—shingles, stress-induced Bell's palsy, near blindness—she failed to take the most basic actions to protect me. I told her repeatedly: file the lawsuit. She refused.

This email stands as a damning record of what it looks like when a client is not only abandoned but actively undermined by the very person paid to protect them.

Let it be a warning: not all harm comes from the enemy's side. Sometimes, the worst betrayal is from your own attorney.

From: Stephen Steiner
To: Scott Fisher
Subject: Re: Responding To Your Recent Contact

My attorney was useless; she blamed me for something she failed to do last year. Now the HOA refuses to fix the problem. They wanted another exterminator to come over, make another hole, and have me wait another three months. This is their game—to keep extending the issue.

Because of the stress, I have been sick for two years and recently got Bell's palsy. Half my face is paralyzed, and I get shingles constantly.

For some reason, my lawyer was never aggressive. She knew their lawyers, and I feel she wasn't representing me well. For a year, all she did was send them a couple of letters. I literally handed her a case that would be impossible to lose. She had the nerve to tell me to get therapy!

I can't sell until it's fixed, and I won't pay for something that's their responsibility. It states in the CCRs that everything above the ceiling is HOA responsibility.

Please call me if you can help or know someone who can.

From: Stephen Steiner
To: Scott Fisher
Subject: Question

Is there a way to find out if my lawyer was purposely sabotaging me? She knows the other lawyers, and I have been thinking of situations that don't make sense. I told her many times to file a lawsuit, and she never would.

I will not pay to fix the crawlspace because it is not my property. That falls under HOA responsibility.

This is the last email she sent me. All nonsense. She never took action. Why would I contact them? That's what I hired her for.

I don't want to pay a single cent to fix this condo. It is all their fault, and they made me suffer for two years. I have had so many medical issues that I want to sue them for millions.

Please call me. I just want your legal knowledge and opinion. Is this normal?

From: Scott Fisher
To: Stephen Steiner
Subject: Re: Question

I'm working on a deadline today, but I'll call you when I free up tomorrow. If I can call this evening, I will.

My quick reaction: It's very unlikely your attorney is purposely sabotaging your case. Your remedies seem limited to mediation first.

Do you feel your attorney agrees with your position that the HOA is responsible? She seems to ask you to cooperate with the HOA's inspection efforts.

Perhaps she can ask the HOA to pay for accessing the crawlspace and repairing any holes made for access. I think it needs to be established that the HOA takes responsibility.

I don't recommend changing attorneys unless you feel it's pointless to continue with her. If so, you should find another local attorney specializing in HOA disputes.

From: Stephen Steiner
To: Scott Fisher
Subject: Re: Question

Thanks for getting back to me. It will be easier to explain over the phone. My lawyer is not aggressive with them. I have been patient and allowed all exterminators in to do whatever was necessary.

Call me if you can tonight or tomorrow. I am so nervous that I will get screwed again.

Any advice would be greatly appreciated.

From: Stephen Steiner
To: Rhona S. Kauffman
Subject: Re: Telephone Conference

I am going to end the contract. The crawlspace is property of the HOA. It is their decision if they choose to rid the crawlspace of rodents and repair the damage. I was stupid to think they cared.

I will not cover the cost or be responsible for repairs to HOA property.

From: Rhona S. Kauffman
To: Stephen Steiner
Subject: Re: Telephone Conference

Hey, this is completely different from what we discussed on the phone. I'm confused—are you now changing your mind?

From: Stephen Steiner
To: Rhona S. Kauffman
Subject: Re: Telephone Conference

They closed the ticket, so I will not allow anyone into my condo. I don't have the funds or energy to play their stupid game. It is their property; if they want to clean it, they will have to relocate me or do it from the roof.

I should have sold as soon as Seabreeze took over management. They are a horrible company.

Sorry for all the drama.

Communication with Rhona ceased after she advised me over the phone to seek therapy, use my own funds to repair HOA-owned property, and concluded with the statement: "there was never really a case."

While I did require therapy—due to the prolonged trauma inflicted by the HOA's gross negligence and Rhona's dismissive, harmful handling of my case—her recommendation that I personally pay for the repair of property legally owned by the HOA was both unethical and legally indefensible. That advice alone reflects a serious breach of fiduciary duty and a fundamental misunderstanding (or willful misrepresentation) of California common-interest development law.

Her claim that "there was never really a case" flies in the face of the months of documented evidence, expert assessments, and her own written acknowledgment of the severe contamination. This statement was not just dishonest—it was calculated and cruel.

A few months later, while browsing the internet, I happened to search for Rhona Kauffman's LinkedIn profile—a page I had attempted to locate multiple times while she was representing me without success. Mysteriously, it became publicly viewable only after she closed out our contract. What I discovered was a revelation: Rhona Kauffman was employed at Guralnick & Gilliland LLP—the same firm representing the HOA—from December 2008 to January 2013.

This was a clear conflict of interest that she had a legal and ethical obligation to disclose. She never did. This omission now explains everything: the constant delays, the refusal to escalate, the failure to submit evidence, the passive-aggressive behavior, and the eventual abandonment of my case. Her conduct wasn't just negligent—it was deceptive, self-serving, and in direct violation of her duty of loyalty to me as her client.

No correspondence from Rhona, HOA, Exterminators,
or Seabreeze throughout the entire month of April.

Mo	Tu	We	Th	Fr	Sa	Su
		1	2	3	4	5
6	7	8	9	10	11	12
13	14	15	16	17	18	19
20	21	22	23	24	25	26
27	28	29	30	31		

MAY

688 DAYS UNRESOLVED

A SPECIAL PLACE

From: Stephen Steiner
  To: Darren Zetena
Subject: Hello

MAY 17, 2024 / 4:08 PM

I want to sell my property. The Palms has become a horrible place for me, and I no longer consider it home.

The crawlspace has to be cleaned before I can sell. My Realtor requires documentation of its completion. At this point, I will accept the sanitization spray. The three openings that were made need to be repaired. Donna assured me it would be taken care of.

Your assistance would be greatly appreciated.

From: Darren Zetena
  To: Stephen Steiner
Subject: RE: The Palms - Steiner, Unit #808 - Rodent Clean-up Email 05-17-2024

MAY 17, 2024 / 5:18 PM

Thank you for the email. I will review your inquiry with the Board of Directors and follow up with you.

From: Stephen Steiner
  To: Bruce Carmichael
Subject: Re: Recommended Vendors

MAY 18, 2024 / 7:57 PM

Wanted to give you an update since your inspection.

My lawyer threw me under the bus. I emailed my attorney two days before the inspection to let her know I was getting one done. She responded "Perfect!" to the email, and I was sure this would finally end the battle. I immediately emailed the report to her the second I received it from you. I asked her to confirm receipt. She knew it was coming, so I didn't think twice about it. Nevertheless, I emailed four more times over the week to confirm and never heard back. Calling was pointless since she never answered or messaged.

Because of this, the HOA attorneys used the silence as a reason to close the case, and I was left with the responsibility. My attorney blamed me because she did not "receive" the email. Strange when she knew it was coming, let alone the confirmation emails sent to her. She then told me to seek therapy and that I should pay to fix the crawlspace. Funny thing, the crawlspace is HOA property. Why would I pay to fix their property?

My theory is she was working with them against me because she slipped earlier in the year and told me she was friends with their attorneys. Looking back, there were signs she was not working for me. She had never come to my condo to see firsthand. She never contacted me unless I did first. Texting and emails were rarely answered, and with all the evidence, this was a slam dunk case. How she lost it is beyond me.

I know this is a long shot, but if you or anyone that can help either with legal or the city, I would appreciate it. I have tried the city but can never get a response from them.

I appreciate any help you can offer.

From: Bruce Carmichael
  To: Stephen Steiner
Subject: Re: Recommended Vendors

MAY 19, 2024 / 1:08 PM

Stephen, sorry about this. I would first file a complaint with the State Bar. I don't know of any attorneys to call for this. It's difficult with HOAs—they have all the money and support and they stonewall you and everyone.

You could file a small claims action against the HOA to get some money and have them pay someone to take the ceilings down and clean up the mess.

A SPECIAL PLACE

From: Stephen Steiner   MAY 20, 2024 / 4:03 AM
    To: Bruce Carmichael
Subject: Re: Recommended Vendors

Thanks for the info. I will contact the State Bar. Everything seems suspicious, and what's the worst that can happen?

I will not do anything involving the HOA. Once I sell, I will never purchase another home. My days of ownership are over. Seems like HOAs are everywhere, and I will avoid them like the rats (which, as I am typing this email, are above my head chewing on something).

(See p. 76)

Mo	Tu	We	Th	Fr	Sa	Su
					~~1~~	~~2~~
~~3~~	~~4~~	~~5~~	~~6~~	~~7~~	~~8~~	~~9~~
~~10~~	~~11~~	12	~~13~~	14	~~15~~	16
~~17~~	~~18~~	19	20	~~21~~	22	23
~~24~~	~~25~~	~~26~~	~~27~~	28	29	30

JUNE

718 DAYS
UNRESOLVED

From: Stephen Steiner
To: Darren Zetena
Subject: Re: The Palms - Steiner, Unit #808 - Rodent Clean-up Email 05-17-2024

JUNE 2, 2024 / 4:38 PM

Any word from the Board? Spoke to my realtor and the condo needs to be cleaned properly. According to the inspection report, it must be gutted and everything replaced, and all wiring checked.

Please contact me if you need a copy of the inspection.

From: Stephen Steiner
To: Darren Zetena
Subject: Hello

JUNE 4, 2024 / 6:37 PM

Not sure why the Board has not responded. I am sure they have painted me as the crazy homeowner who was uncooperative and difficult. I endured years of exterminators coming into my unit, making holes in my ceiling, and accomplishing nothing. I was treated horribly by the HOA and Seabreeze. The HOA is there to help, not hurt. Not once did anyone call, stop by, or ask how I was during this entire ordeal. The fact that I am living in a rat-infested condo should have been a great concern to everyone.

Donna and Shelley did nothing to remedy the situation. Making holes in my ceiling and setting traps in the crawlspace does nothing. I do not want any more holes in my ceiling. Put the traps on the roof and catch them before they get in. There is so much feces and urine-soaked insulation my unit reeks of it. When rats run across the ceiling, it sounds like hail falling. The insulation is so saturated by urine that it is running down the walls.

I have suffered for so long. The fungus, welts, shingles, and Bell's Palsy from inhaling this toxic air for three years is unforgivable. Even the exterminators the HOA hired said I should not be living in the condo.

I cannot sell until the HOA repairs all the damage done. The lawyer I hired was useless. The crawlspace is not my property. The HOA has to pay for the repair. Would any of them like to live in my condo? If any Board Member were living in this unit, it would have been resolved immediately.

I will be happy to forward the documents & videos or even stop by if someone would actually enter my condo and see firsthand. Please let me know.

From: Marilyn Ramos
To: Stephen Steiner
CC: Wayne Guralnick
Subject: THE PALMS HOA

JUNE 6, 2024 / 12:46 PM

See attached.

From: Stephen Steiner
To: Marilyn Ramos
Subject: Re: THE PALMS HOA

JUNE 6, 2024 / 4:38 PM

The HOA hired three extermination companies who never located the access point over a two-year period. Not one of them offered to do a smoke test to locate the opening. Setting traps in the crawlspace is pointless. They should have set them on the roof. I told Donna this in the very beginning. Trap them before they get into the crawlspace.

I refused because setting traps did nothing. Set the traps in other units. Let homeowners experience what I had to endure. Maybe they will enjoy years of sleepless nights, the stench of urine and feces, and the countless number of exterminators entering their unit.

I already know they have no empathy for human life.

GURALNICK & GILLILAND, LLP
ATTORNEYS AT LAW

A FULL SERVICE COMMUNITY
ASSOCIATION LAW FIRM

40-004 COOK STREET, SUITE 3
PALM DESERT, CALIFORNIA 92211
TELEPHONE: (760) 340-1515
FACSIMILE: (760) 568-3053
E-MAIL: WAYNEG@GGHOALAW.COM

PLEASE REFER TO FILE: 84-260

June 6, 2024

SENT VIA EMAIL (ssteiner.la@gmail.com)
Stephen Steiner
3155 E. Ramon Road
#808
Palm Springs, CA

> **Re:** **The Palms Homeowners Association ("Association") - Your Request for Further Work to be Performed at Unit #808 ("Subject Unit")**

Mr. Steiner:

We understand that you are no longer represented by counsel. As you know, this office is corporate counsel to the Association. We are advised that you wish to sell the Subject Unit and want the Association to perform further work at said Subject Unit.

The Association stands by its last communication to attorney Kauffman, a copy of which is enclosed herein and made a part hereof by this reference.

Sincerely,

GURALNICK & GILLILAND, LLP

Wayne Guralnick

Wayne Guralnick
/mr

Encl.
cc: Association

S:\84-260\Letters\Steiner.Letter.060624.wpd

From: Stephen Steiner
To: Marilyn Ramos
Subject: Re: THE PALMS HOA

JUNE 14, 2024 / 3:19 PM

I took a week to reflect on this issue.

The fact that the HOA is basing my decision to decline another exterminator to repeat a pointless process is moot. The only people I will allow to enter my condo are those that are going to repair the damage. Here are the facts:

> The crawlspace is managed by the HOA.
> The crawlspace is HOA property as written in the CCRs.
> The crawlspace will be repaired by the HOA.

As to the duties of the Association:

Operation and Maintenance of Common Area and Recreation Area.

To operate, maintain, and otherwise manage or provide for the operation, maintenance, and management of the common area and all its facilities, improvements, and landscaping, including any other property acquired by the Association, in a first-class condition and in a good state of repair.

When repairs are completed, exterminators are free to set traps on the roof. Trapping them before they enter the building is a better solution.

How the HOA and Seabreeze have twisted this to make it my responsibility is disgusting. Everyone knows they are at fault. I have bent over backwards to have this resolved. Nothing has been resolved. I have lived in a toxic environment for three years.

From: Stephen Steiner
To: Darren Zetena
Subject: Question

JUNE 18, 2024 / 5:20 PM

I am attaching my home inspection report that my former attorney never sent to the HOA even though she confirmed receipt and that she would send it immediately.

This is for your records. It shows how bad my condo is. Not sure why nothing has been done. It is dangerous for a human to live in conditions like this.

I am also attaching a page from the report supplied by the exterminators the HOA hired. I have gotten all of the signs. Please let the HOA know that what they are doing is against the law. The crawlspace is their property, and they need to clean up the mess. This issue is getting bigger and bigger the longer they do nothing.

I have been living with this for three years.

If this was your condo, would you allow this? I welcome you to come to my condo and experience what I go through every day.

From: Darren Zetena
To: Stephen Steiner
Subject: RE: The Palms - Steiner, Unit 808 - Email Question 06-18-2024

JUNE 18, 2024 / 7:48 PM

This is to confirm receipt. I will review your inquiry with the Board.

A SPECIAL PLACE

Thank you, Darren.

Not sure why the HOA is treating me this way. The money spent on the pickleball courts should have gone towards the rat problem this complex is experiencing. Do they not understand how dangerous it is to live in this toxic environment? Ask Shelley if she would like to live this way.

Legally, they must maintain the common areas.

Do they understand what damage they are doing to the building and to my health and life? The stress caused my shingles to get so bad that I got Bell's Palsy. Now I can barely see out of my right eye, and half my face is numb. This is all because of them.

They made this issue personal. They did nothing to fix this issue but dragged it out for years. I want to sell and move. They are legally required to maintain the common areas. As long as they can have a company clean the crawlspace and show documentation that it has been completed, I can put my unit on the market.

Let the HOA know how wonderful it was to move back to The Palms after my partner passed and, three months later, my mother. Dealing with these issues every single day, day and night. I would trade homes with any of them so they could experience the nightmare they put me through.

They are the ones who made me what I am today.

I hope they are pleased with their work.

Last night, a rat got trapped in one of the old sticky traps. I got zero sleep, and he finally died on top of the access hole that was made two years ago.

I have no clue who takes care of this. It is in HOA property, so I assume the HOA.

If not, I guess I will have to deal with it.

I am attaching thermal images of the wall in my second bedroom and the laundry room ceiling (the white spot is the rat). This is what I am living in. Apparently, the HOA does not take this issue seriously.

Sorry for all the trouble. It should have never gotten this bad.

I would like to send out Jordan with Preferred Pest Control to assess the situation.

May I have your permission to send them out to inspect your home?

Yes, please.

A SPECIAL PLACE

From: Darren Zetena
   To: Stephen Steiner
Subject: RE: The Palms - Steiner, Unit 808 - Rat -2nd Bedroom-Laundry Room (W/O #31285)

A work order has been issued, and a phone call was placed with the pest control contractor.

From: Stephen Steiner
   To: Darren Zetena
Subject: Re: The Palms - Steiner, Unit #808 - Rat -2nd Bedroom-Laundry Room (W/O #31285)

Thank you.

Sorry you have to deal with me and this issue. The Board ruined my life over rats. I am trying everything I can think of to get the condo on the market so I can leave this prison they put me in. Why did they spend all that money on the pickleball courts and not on this issue? It is toxic for me to live in this.

Next time you are at the complex, please stop by. I need at least one person from Seabreeze to experience it.

From: Darren Zetena
   To: Stephen Steiner
Subject: RE: The Palms - Steiner, Unit #808 - Rat -2nd Bedroom-Laundry Room (W/O #31285)

I have spoken with Jordan, the pest control technician. He will be contacting you to coordinate coming to your home.

Mo	Tu	We	Th	Fr	Sa	Su
~~1~~	~~2~~	~~3~~	~~4~~	~~5~~	~~6~~	~~7~~
~~8~~	~~9~~	10	11	12	13	14
15	16	~~17~~	18	19	20	21
22	23	24	~~25~~	~~26~~	27	~~28~~
~~29~~	30	~~31~~				

JULY

749 DAYS
UNRESOLVED

A SPECIAL PLACE

From: Darren Zetena
To: Stephen Steiner
Subject: HIGH PRIORITY: The Palms - Steiner, Unit #808 - Electrical Inspection

I wanted to see if you are available for an electrical inspection of your unit on Thursday, July 18, 2024, between 8:00 AM and 9:00 AM. I would be present with the electrician during the inspection.

Please let me know as soon as possible of your availability.

From: Stephen Steiner
To: Darren Zetena
Subject: Re: HIGH PRIORITY: The Palms - Steiner, Unit #808 - Electrical Inspection

JULY 12, 2024 / 12:58 PM

I am available.

Thank you for being the only person to help me with this. Appreciate it very much.

From: Darren Zetena
To: Stephen Steiner
Subject: RE: HIGH PRIORITY: The Palms - Steiner, Unit #808 - Electrical Inspection

JULY 12, 2024 / 12:59 PM

Perfect. Thank you. I will coordinate with Horizon Lighting. We will see you on Thursday, 07-18-2024, between 8:00 AM and 9:00 AM.

CLOSED FILE

From: Rhona S. Kauffman
To: Stephen Steiner
Subject: Closed File

DECEMBER 8, 2024 / 7:35 PM

Stephen,

Good evening. Attached is the last invoice from March 2024, and as you know, I never heard back from you after that.

I assume you wanted your file closed since you never responded.

I do not know whether you allowed for the second phase of the pest control project or whether you hired an expert to handle anything on your behalf.

I do know you were very frustrated with the process that needed to be followed, and I understand it was very overwhelming for you.

I have closed your file and wrote off the balance owed since I never heard back from you.

Please let me know if you have any questions or comments or need my assistance.

I hope you are doing better and can enjoy the holidays.

Sincerely,
Rhona S. Kauffman, Esq.
LAW OFFICES OF RHONA S. KAUFFMAN

It's remarkable how you assumed I wanted my case closed. No, Rhona—please keep it open so you can not fight for me.

'Need your assistance?'

That's laughable. You've already destroyed everything I worked so hard to build. If this is what you consider legal representation, perhaps it's time you revisit the fundamentals of what it means to be an attorney and an advocate. Because what you provided was neither.

A SPECIAL PLACE

After everything I endured at the hands of Rhona Kauffman, Shelley Westall, Donna Rickman, the HOA Board of Directors, and the exterminators they employed, I was left with no choice but to sever all contact with my abusers. These individuals systematically destroyed my life, my health, and my financial stability. What they did was not simply negligent—it was calculated, malicious, and inhumane.

This entire ordeal was orchestrated by Shelley Westall, who used Donna, Rhona, and Seabreeze Management as pawns in her campaign to ensure the HOA would not pay for the cleanup and repairs of their own property. Their coordinated strategy forced me—an innocent homeowner—into a prolonged nightmare of toxic exposure, psychological torment, and financial ruin, all to protect their own liability.

Seabreeze Management, in particular, had a legal and ethical duty to intervene. As the property management company, they were responsible for protecting the safety and wellbeing of residents. Given the overwhelming evidence that my condo was toxic and uninhabitable, they should have immediately relocated me and arranged for proper remediation. Their complete inaction was not just negligent—it was reckless and malicious. Their failure to fulfill their duty has now opened the door for legal action.

What makes this even more unbearable is this was my home. It was supposed to be my sanctuary, my investment, my safe place filled with memories of the life I built with my partner. Instead, it became a sealed tomb infested with rats and cruelty. For over three years, I was forced to live in a contaminated environment so dangerous it triggered constant outbreaks of shingles, severe depression, fungal infections, tooth extractions, Bell's palsy, and permanent partial blindness in one eye. I lost my health, my dignity, my sanity—and eventually, I lost everything.

The psychological abuse was just as brutal. I became isolated and withdrawn. Friends distanced themselves, unaware or unwilling to acknowledge the horror I was enduring. The humiliation, anger, and desperation they pushed me into became visible. I know how they spoke about me. I know how they laughed. The smirking email typos, the feigned confusion, the never-ending gaslighting—these weren't coincidences. They were the calling cards of people who saw my suffering as a source of entertainment and a problem to be erased, not solved.

Rhona Kauffman—who I later discovered worked for the HOA's legal counsel—never represented me. She betrayed me. She delayed, deflected, and ultimately participated in my destruction. Whether she was compensated for her betrayal or simply blinded by loyalty to her former employer, I'll never know. But what's clear is that her actions violated every tenet of legal ethics and professional integrity.

The end result? I was forced to personally fund the biohazard cleanup of the HOA's crawlspace—property I did not own and had no legal responsibility for. I had to sell my home at a loss just to escape the torture they inflicted. The cleanup team, horrified by what they found, documented the conditions in detail. The entire crawlspace was soaked in rat, feces, and urine. That was the environment I was forced to live in, day after day, while these people—who had a legal and moral duty to act—did nothing.

CONGRATULATIONS, SHELLEY.

BRAVO, DONNA.

WELL PLAYED, RHONA.

If your goal was to break me, to silence me, to destroy my life—you succeeded. But know this: your names are now tied to the truth. This book exists as a record of what you did and who you really are. And I hope every person who reads it— your friends, your families, your colleagues—sees you for what you are: abusers hiding behind HOA titles, management companies, and legal degrees.

I lost everything. But I will not lose my voice. And I will not let you erase what you did.

WARNING:
THE IMAGES BELOW CONTAIN GRAPHIC CONTENT THAT MAY BE DEEPLY DISTURBING OR NAUSEATING. THIS WAS NOT AN ISOLATED ISSUE— THESE CONDITIONS EXISTED DIRECTLY ABOVE MY HEAD, SPANNING THE ENTIRE CONDO. I WAS FORCED TO LIVE LIKE THIS FOR THREE YEARS.

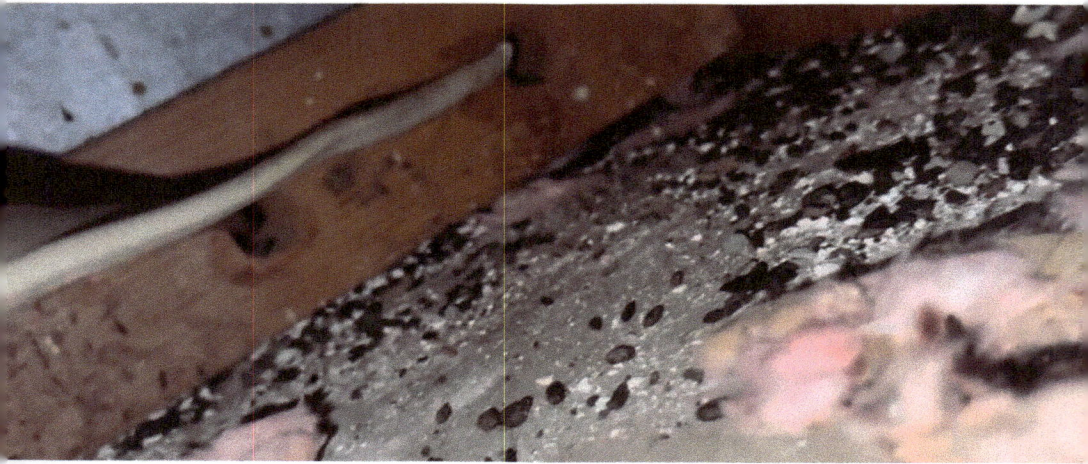

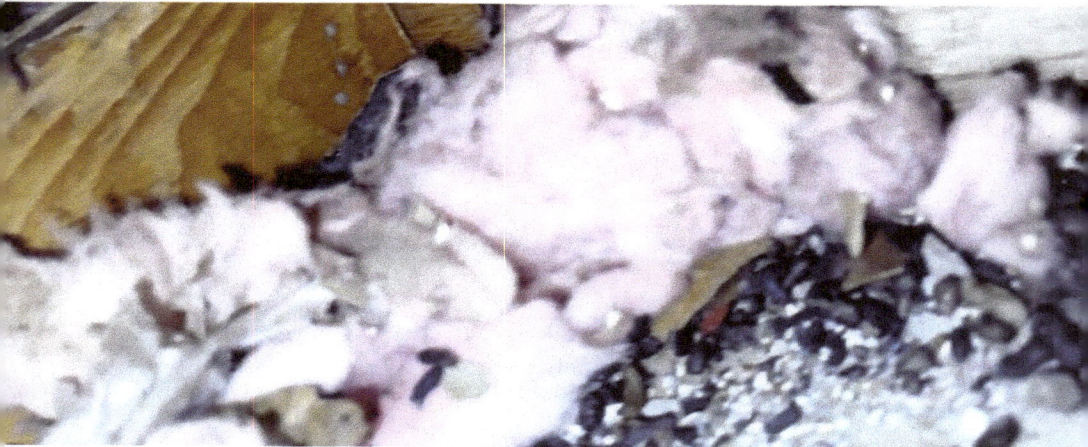

ENTIRE KITCHEN CRAWLSPACE FILLED WITH RODENT FECES

DRYWALL AND INSULATION SOAKED WITH URINE AND FECES

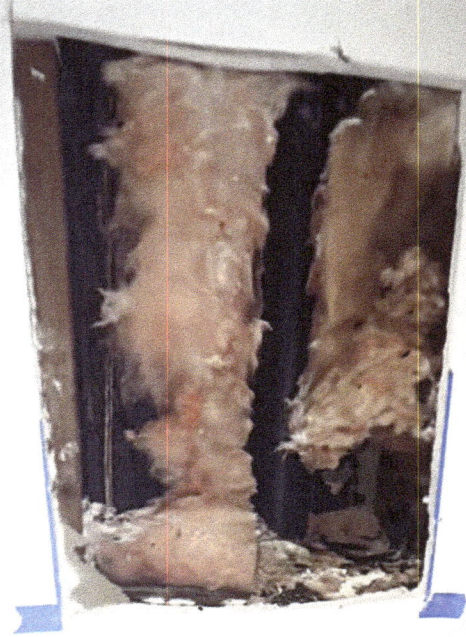

DAMAGE FROM RODENTS THROUGHOUT ENTIRE CONDO

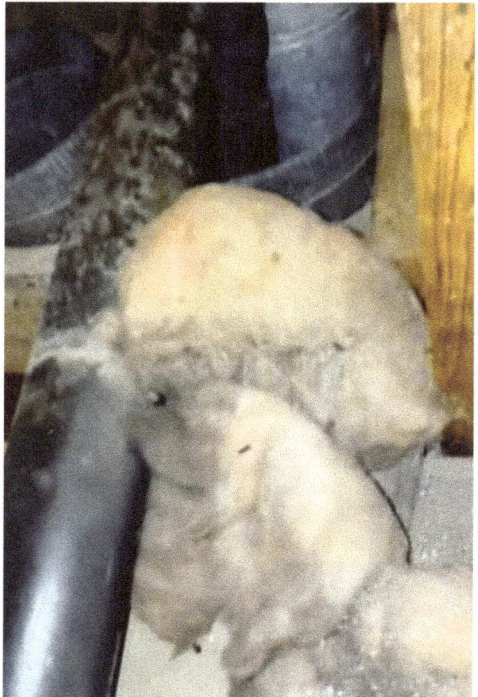

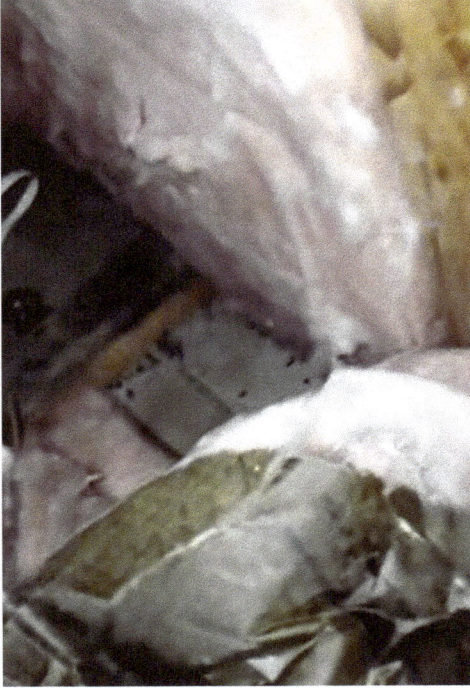

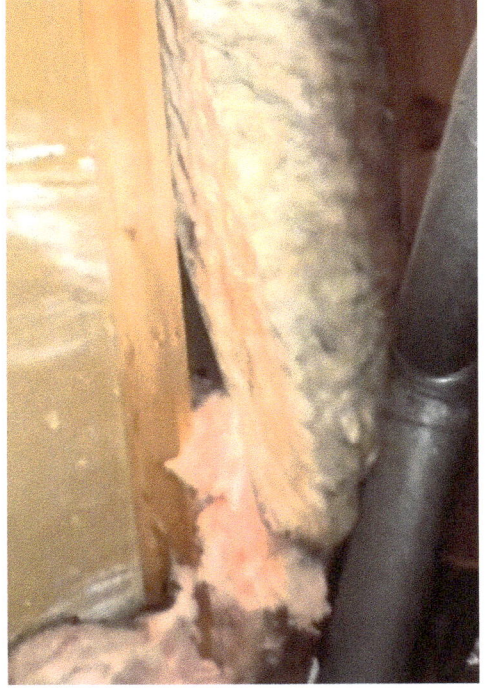

ENTIRE CRAWLSPACE WAS CONTAMINATED WITH URINE AND FECES

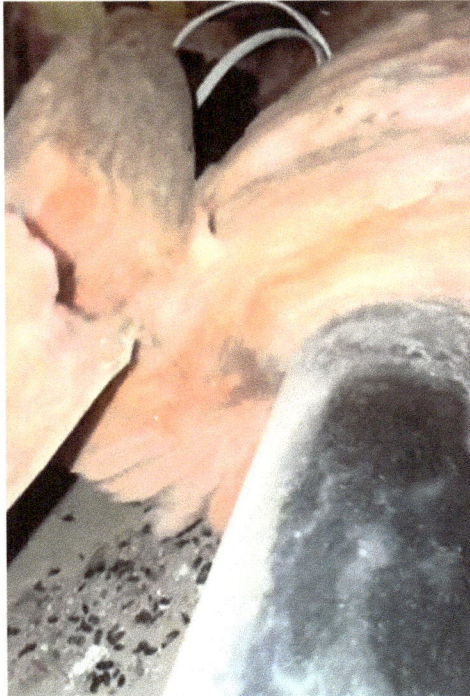

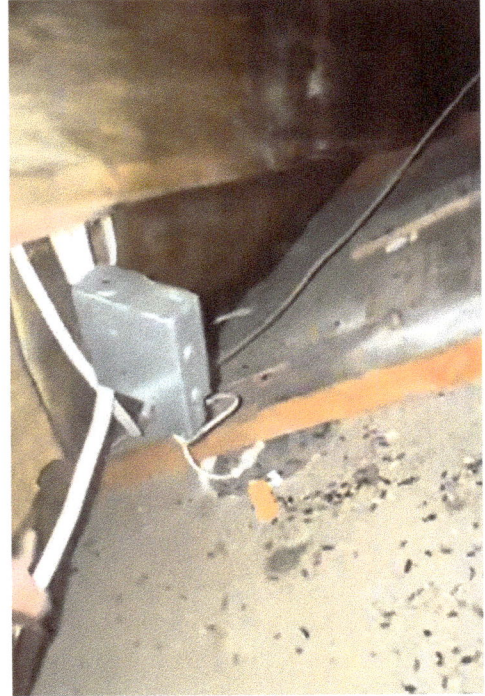

in

| Articles | People | Learning | Jobs | Games |

stand for justice

Rhona S. Kauffman, Esq.

Business Owner at Law Offices of Rhona S. Kauffman

San Diego, California, United States · Contact Info

2K followers · 500+ connections

See your mutual connections

Join to view profile   ◄ Message

Law Offices of Rhona S. Kauffman

Whittier Law School

Company Website

Services

Startup Law   Real Estate   Business Law   Consumer Law   Corporate Law   Legal Consulting

Estate Planning Law   Trust and Estate Litigation

RHONA S. KAUFFMAN LINKEDIN RESUME

Experience

Business Owner

Law Offices of Rhona S. Kauffman

Dec 1993 - Present · 31 years 4 months

77564 Country Club Dr. Suite 115 Palm Desert, CA 92211

* Since 1994, specializing in Civil Litigation; Business Law; Real Estate Law;
Corporate Formation and Partnership Disputes; Insurance Litigation; Homeowners
Associations, All Transactional preparation of Agreements/Contracts, and Estate
Planning Living Trusts Wills

* Originally from Los Angeles, serving San Diego County; Riverside County including
Palm Desert and San Bernardino County since 1996. www.rhonakauffmanlaw.com
(760) 772-8225

*TOP LAWYER AWARD: Palm Springs Life...

Show more

Attorney

Guralnick & Gilliland, LLP

Dec 2008 - Jan 2013 · 4 years 2 months

Palm Desert, California

Real Estate Litigation, Construction Defects, Homeowers Association Law, Business
and Corporate litigation

Attorney

Joseph A. Gibbs & Associates

Aug 2004 - Dec 2008 · 4 years 5 months

Indian Wells, California

Real Estate, Business, Employment law, Corporate litigation and Transcational
including formation of business entities.

CONFLICT OF INTEREST

This was a clear and undeniable conflict of interest—one she was both ethically and legally obligated to disclose. Had I known the truth, I never would have hired her, and I would have ended the contract immediately. Placing my trust in her became the most devastating mistake of my life—emotionally, legally, and financially. I lost not only my home and health, but also a significant portion of the savings I worked a lifetime to build. Though I hope to recover, the damage is profound, and at my age, I fear the time and resources to rebuild may no longer be there."

SIDE NOTE

Many may wonder why I didn't take my story to the press—why I didn't contact newspapers, television stations, radio shows, or other media outlets.

The truth is, I did.

I reached out to all of them, multiple times. Not a single one returned my calls or responded to my emails. It was as if I didn't exist.

My suffering was invisible, and my voice was ignored—just like it had been by the HOA, Seabreeze Management, and everyone else who had the power to intervene but chose not to.

On March 4th, 2025, I was forced to undergo yet another dental extraction— this time the molar directly beneath the previously removed molar—after it was discovered to be cracked clean through during a routine cleaning.

To this day, the effects of Bell's palsy still linger on one side of my face. I live with permanent scarring from shingles, flare ups whenever stress returns, and the vision in my right eye continues to worsen.

Who could have imagined that a single email would set off a chain of events that destroyed everything I had built.

ACKNOWLEDGMENTS

To the few friends who stood by me while everything else collapsed—thank you. Your compassion, loyalty, and humanity during the darkest and most isolating chapter of my life will never be forgotten. You were a lifeline when everything else—my health, home, livelihood, and hope—was being stripped away.

To those who walked away, or chose to believe gossip instead of seeking truth—perhaps you judged what you didn't understand. But unless you've lived for years beneath a ceiling infested with rats, breathing contaminated air, enduring psychological torture, medical trauma, and being systematically ignored while your life crumbles around you, you simply have no frame of reference. This wasn't "just a condo." It was my safe place. It was the final piece of the life I had built with my partner. Watching it rot while I begged for help shattered something inside me that may never fully heal.

To every person who knew of my suffering and remained silent—to the neighbors, the bystanders, and the indifferent officials—you saw what was happening. You knew I was living in toxic, hazardous conditions. You saw the toll it took on my body and mind. And still, you did nothing. No outreach. No calls to the city, the health department, the media. Nothing. You watched me drown and turned away.

To the Palms HOA, the Board of Directors, Seabreeze Management, and the exterminators who admitted the health hazards yet left me behind—you are legally and morally complicit. You failed to uphold your duty of care. Instead of intervening, you conspired in my prolonged exposure to a toxic, uninhabitable environment, violating not only your contractual obligations but basic standards of decency and California health and safety codes.

To Rhona Kauffman, my retained counsel, who failed to disclose her previous employment with the HOA's law firm, obstructed communication, and ultimately abandoned her legal responsibilities—you betrayed the very oath you swore to uphold. Your conflict of interest, lack of advocacy, and dereliction of duty weren't just unethical—they are grounds for disciplinary action. You were supposed to fight for me. Instead, you joined them.

To Shelley Westall and Donna Rickman—you didn't just fail to act. You orchestrated this. You deliberately prolonged my suffering in what appears to be a calculated attempt to avoid HOA liability and force me from my home. You succeeded. You broke me—mentally, physically, financially. Your actions were not administrative missteps. They were cruel, targeted, and inexcusable.

And to the law firm of Guralnick & Gilliland—your behavior was no different. You used the flimsiest of excuses to justify abandoning the cleanup: claiming I had failed to contact you to initiate Phase 2 of the rodent exclusion, a responsibility that legally and contractually fell on Rhona Kauffman, not me. After two years of utter inaction, I declined yet another visit from an exterminator who intended to make yet another hole and set yet more traps—because it was obvious the entire process had become a staged performance to delay, deflect, and gaslight.

You all knew exactly what you were doing. You should have relocated me immediately, investigated properly, and resolved the issue without exposing me to further harm. But you didn't. You left me to rot in a contaminated unit, knowing it was toxic and uninhabitable. You ignored every exterminator's warning. You ignored every cry for help. And you laughed behind the scenes while I unraveled.

Rhona Kauffman, Shelley Westall, Donna Rickman, and Wyane Guralnick —what you engaged in wasn't just negligence. It was psychological warfare. It was torture. And you should all be held criminally liable for what you did to me. You deserve to be investigated, exposed, disbarred—and imprisoned. You destroyed my life.

The psychological toll has been devastating. Shingles, Bell's palsy, permanent vision damage, tooth loss, and emotional collapse—these were the costs of your collective inaction and cruelty. But the destruction didn't stop with my health. You financially devastated me. You forced me out of my home—my only source of stability—and left me no choice but to sell my property, my investment, at a massive loss. You took everything I had worked for and left me homeless. I now live with chronic trauma, grief, and isolation. I am not who I once was.

I am a different person. One you created. Not one I chose.

I've included these photos to silence any further questions about the condition of my home's interior. Had Shelley Westall, Rhona Kauffman, or Wayne Guralnick taken even an hour out of their schedules to personally step inside my unit, they would have seen the truth for themselves. The filth wasn't mine—it was theirs, festering above my head in the crawlspace they were responsible for maintaining.

What's even more disgraceful is that Donna Rickman did see the interior. She knew exactly how clean my home was, yet apparently said nothing to stop the false narrative. Instead, they doubled down—insulting me with an outrageous letter accusing me of living in filth. They knew better. They just didn't care.

Their actions—and their cowardice—destroyed my life. And if there's any justice in this world or the next, there's *a special place* in hell reserved for people who knowingly let others suffer to protect themselves.